Who Is the Minister's Wife?

Who Is the Minister's Wife?

A Search for Personal Fulfillment

Charlotte Ross

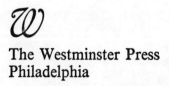

The Westminster Press
Philadelphia

Copyright © 1980 The Westminster Press

First edition

Published by The Westminster Press ®
Philadelphia, Pennsylvania

PRINTED IN THE UNITED STATES OF AMERICA

9 8 7 6 5 4 3 2

Library of Congress Cataloging in Publication Data

Ross, Charlotte, 1921–
  Who is the minister's wife?

  Bibliography: p.
  1. Clergymen's wives. I. Title
BV4395.R67   248'.4   79-24027
ISBN 0-664-24302-9

Contents

Preface

She can be seen in countless magazines, on billboards, or strolling the shopping malls of suburbia. She can be found behind a typewriter or an executive's desk. She may be deep in a mine or high on a telephone pole. She may be driving a truck or trying a case in court. She is, in fact, involved in every facet of life. She is the American Woman.

One advertisement states, "You've come a long way, baby." As one looks at the long record of human history, one sees that indeed she has. Her changing advancement is impressive. She is the envy of women throughout the world for her standard of living, her significant gains in education, her economic affluence, and her physical health.

Still the American woman is not fully content. She continues to seek fulfillment and equality, not only in the job market but also behind the closed doors of her own home. She is searching for her own personhood in its deepest sense as she asks the questions: Who am I? Where am I going? and Why?

In the past, American women primarily filled the role of homemaker. The earliest settlers faced a vast, untamed frontier in a land of hazard and hardship. The women of Colonial America made homes from whatever came handy. As the nation moved westward it was the presence of the wives of the settlers that often spelled the difference between a lawless, brawling frontier town and a settled productive community. Her role bound her with all other women, since childbearing was similar in cabin and in mansion, and the responsibilities of nurture and nutrition were a common thread running through daily life. These things she was expected to do while the men earned the livelihood.

Discrimination against women based on legal precedents dates back to the beginnings of Western law itself. Classic Athenian and Roman law categorized women on the same level as slaves, and during the Dark Ages they were considered chattel. Under English common law and eventually in the United States, a woman had no equality under the law apart from her husband. As a result, the average woman was often trapped in a role not of her own design. With no available choice, she did what she had to do—she followed her mother into a career that was grounded on the kitchen, the church, and the cradle.

Consequently, the American woman held a second-class status granted by myth, law, social custom, and her own undefined self. There are various answers given as to when significant change began to occur. Some point to the abolitionist movement in the early 1800's as the time when women emerged as a political force. In 1848, the Women's Rights Convention demanded the vote, equal opportunity in jobs and education, and an end to legal discrimination based on sex. These claims went unheeded for scores of years. It was not until 1920, with ratification of the Nineteenth Amendment, that women finally got the right to vote.

During the 1930's, women began to attend college in increasing numbers, looking toward careers in the professions. World War II brought in a folk figure, Rosie the Riveter, a symbol of the many women who entered the work force and liked the independence gained by working. In our own time, technology has made brawn less important in the labor force, better education has broadened woman's vision beyond home duties, the increased health and declining birthrate has meant more time free from childbearing and child-rearing, and medical science has developed a longer life expectancy.

Along with these realities, the civil rights movement, while scoring gains for black Americans, produced a new awareness by other second-class citizens, among them the American Woman. With a new consciousness of personal aspirations beyond those boundaries set by the male, the American woman struggles to find the self she believes is there. A new woman is emerging who, perhaps for the first time, is a creation of female imagination. She encompasses a broader state of mind that asks new and serious questions about marriage, family life, jobs, power, and the nature of men and women themselves.

The American woman who has married a clergyman shares the struggle for full equality. Such a new partnership calls for a careful balancing of obligation, privilege, and role fulfillment. However, the minister's wife carries additional baggage with her into the encounter.

The role of "clergy wife" is difficult to portray, since it is played against a diverse backdrop. It is as individual as each woman, but a composite can be drawn, since, in spite of differences, there is some common ground. Wives of clergymen are a definable group within a developed and developing role. The changing nature of that role has occasioned tension, struggle, and rewards. It has affected and continues to affect the minister, his family, and the church itself.

A magazine devoted to church administration states that disturbing reports are emerging from denominational executives concerning the depth of unhappiness and frustration among clergy wives, and a growing divorce rate among men in the ministry. Denominational headquarters and inter-church agencies have only begun to study the problem and its implications. The Task Force on Women of the Synod of the Trinity, a middle judicatory of The United Presbyterian Church in the U.S.A., has begun an exploration of this subject. They developed and circulated questionnaires that sought information from three sources—the clergy wife, the clergyman, and the lay person. By compiling responses from three perspectives, they hoped to gain a balanced profile of the issue and begin to develop some realistic plans for coping with changing needs.

The answers to the questionnaires are, for the most part, thoughtful, frank, and show a depth of feeling and perception which must be admired. They reflect a sense of mission and commitment that is cause for celebration. The list of services to the church, both local and beyond, is staggering. The number of skills and talents of the wives is impressive. Their dedication and zeal is exemplary. Each wife is unique, since each brings her own personality into her own set of circumstances. No single image could ever impart the diversity these wives represent. A significantly interesting picture has emerged from the data. Much of what has happened to women in the rest of society has had an impact on the churches. The problems of the clergy wife, therefore, deserve special study.

I should like to express gratitude to all those who participated in the survey, especially the clergy wives; those persons who, in personal interviews and conversation, shared insights and suggestions; the members of the Task Force on Women for our joint participation as a caring community. My special thanks to my husband, who made me a clergy wife thirty-eight years ago and whose love, counsel, and encouragement have supported my own search for self.

C.R.

Chapter I

It All Began
with Priscilla

It began long ago when Priscilla, the wife of a Jewish tentmaker from Pontus, met the apostle Paul. She was a Roman from an influential family. She and her husband, Aquila, had escaped the persecution of Christians under Claudius. Paul met them at Corinth, and they became partners in a tentmaking firm, while the apostle preached in the synagogue every Sabbath to a mixed company of Jews and Greeks. Priscilla seems to have been educated and well instructed in the Christian gospel. From Corinth Priscilla and her husband moved, with Paul, to Ephesus. There they risked their lives for him in the riots stirred up by the Ephesian worshipers of the goddess Diana.

They established a church in Ephesus and undertook the instruction of Apollos of Alexandria in Christian doctrine. In short, they were embarked upon the Christian ministry. Priscilla may well be the first woman who married a man with one vocation and ended up with a preacher. She was an evangelist in her own right. At any rate, Paul called her a fellow laborer in Christ, and honored her by placing her name before that of her husband. She might very well be the first of a long line of clergy wives who have made a unique contribution to the Christian church.

The line, however, is neither straight nor continuous. Early on, the church developed the tradition of a celibate clergy which many historians perceive grew out of its deep suspicion of the human body, sexuality, and women. Consequently, woman's role in the church was confined to monastic orders where women became the "brides" of their Lord and not of men. The Reformation changed all that when Katherine von Bora became the wife of Martin Luther. She was an exceptional woman and perhaps unconsciously set patterns for the minister's wife that are influential to this day.

She was born in 1499 at Lippendorf and lived there until her mother's death when she was ten years old. Since a relative was the abbess of the convent at Nimbschen and her aunt was a nun there, she entered the convent and at sixteen took the veil as a nun also. In 1519, Katherine heard Luther and other Reformers at Grimma and found herself stirred by their ideas. As news of the Reformation spread, she desired to renounce her vows and leave the convent. With no money and no place to go, this seemed a futile desire. She appealed to Luther for help and on Easter eve in 1523, she and eight other nuns made their escape.

It is a romantic story which reflects her daring. The nuns had all gathered in Katherine's room to await the hour of midnight when they were to make their escape. They were all afraid, not only for themselves but for Leonard Koppe, who was aiding them. The penalty for escaping from a nunnery or aiding in that escape was death.

Leonard brought a big wagon and waited below the window. He had enlisted the help of his nephew and a friend to place the nuns in empty herring barrels on the wagon bed. Their destination, Torgau, was in the territory of a foe of the Reformation who would zealously enforce the law. Fortunately, they were unmolested except for a query by one passerby, "What is in the barrels?" To this Leonard replied,

"Herring," and drove on. The wagon reached Torgau on Easter Tuesday and Katherine found shelter in the home of Phillip Reichenbach.

Nuns who had renounced their vows were encouraged to marry. This appeared to be the best route toward support and security. Consequently, Katherine became engaged to Jerome Baumgartner. When his family objected to an escaped nun, he broke it off. She refused to marry the Reverend Casper Glatz, declaring she would only marry someone she could respect. So on June 13 in a private ceremony and on June 27 in a public ceremony Katherine von Bora became a clergy wife.

Katherine was not handsome. She was, in fact, decidedly plain. But she had a strong face, with a pleasant smile and a warm, welcoming voice. She transformed a bare cloister into an inviting and comfortable home. Her image is of one whose intense interest centered in her husband and his work. She was always in the background, not self-consciously so—as if trying to direct attention away from herself—but naturally, putting other people and interests foremost in her activity.

The wives of the Reformed ministers of Wittenberg organized the Frauenverein, or Ladies Society. Its special mission was to aid the sick and needy, with each woman taking her turn in ministering. In addition, Katherine Luther was the mother of six children and the director of a house that boarded university students. She was a nurse during the plague, at risk to her own health. And above all these she cared for and was supportive of her husband. In all these ways Katherine von Bora Luther developed a role model for subsequent clergy wives that conveyed selflessness, skill, warmth, knowledge, and cooperation.

Little is recorded of the part played by clergy wives in the history of the Reformed churches. No doubt they were strong, effective partners in a significant movement, sharing equally its triumphs and tragedies. The silence of literature simply reflects the status of women generally, and the wives of ministers in particular. In both—the world of society and the world of the church—their service was needed but in an anonymous and supportive way. It is to their credit and is a testimony to the strength of their faith that for the most part they have made a difference in both.

In recent decades change in the role of the clergy wife has accelerated. Let us examine the profiles of three whom I have known.

NAMELESS MRS. SHAW

I didn't know her first name until I read her obituary. She was always, "Mrs. Shaw, the minister's wife" and no one ever called her by her given name. I never thought to wonder why. I just accepted it, as I accepted the fact that Tim our handyman and Sally who did our laundry had no last names. Mrs. Shaw was tall and slender, so she could fill inconspicuous corners and blend with the background. For most folks she was real only as she was a reflection of her husband.

There was no question about his status in the scheme of things. Mrs. Shaw never called him by his first name, either —at least not in public. He had a really important-sounding name, too. The Reverend John Wesley Shaw! It had rhythm and foundation and authority behind it. In conversation she would say, "Reverend Shaw said such and such" or "The Reverend will be officiating at a funeral today." There was a real sense of formality between them—before other people, at least—and I never saw any gesture of affection or physical touching for the congregation to observe. He seemed involved in heavenly issues that set him apart from earthly or earthy contacts. Undoubtedly he was "the Chief" and Mrs. Shaw "the Indian."

They were not at all alike. He was big, with a booming voice that filled the church until he dropped it to a whisper that made you strain to hear what he was saying. Everyone agreed that he was a "real good preacher" and a good man besides.

Those were depression days in the early '30s. Churches dependent on the gifts of members were hard pressed for funds when men were unemployed or poorly paid. Reverend Shaw preached on Sundays, had funerals and weddings, called on the sick, and comforted the sad. That was his real job but it didn't pay much.

It was Mrs. Shaw who was the magician. She had a big garden at the back of the parsonage where she grew tomatoes and peas, potatoes and beans. These made good stews for growing bodies, and gleaming jars of vegetables, fruits, jelly, and pickles that helped to feed the family during the winter season and filled the pantry. Canning was really a necessity, for often bounties of the harvest, or chickens, or eggs were contributed instead of money. Mrs. Shaw would process them for use at another time. She always had some flowers growing along the edges of her garden patch, as if she needed a spot of color in her life. They often found their way to the church on a Sunday or to the table beside a sickbed during the week.

Her life was bound up in the church. The Ladies Sewing Circle, with its mending for the needy and for the missionary barrels, and its quilting for a little money was where she spent her free time.

Mr. Shaw had been a carpenter when they married, able to do most anything in the building trade. He had plenty of opportunity to use his skills in the succession of old, shabby, run-down houses they lived in. Apparently, Mrs. Shaw didn't despair, just made them clean and as warm as possible. Not that she never complained. When she knew that a move was coming she would ask tentatively about the house that went with the charge, sigh and grumble, and flick her dustcloth rebelliously, but in the end she would do her best again. It was just not her place to question an arrangement between the Lord and her husband. He led—she followed, that was the natural order of things.

Nor did she ever expect to take part in the "workings" of the congregation. She baked scores of cakes, mixed gallons of punch and made coffee for the times when the official board or committees of the church met at the parsonage. She was always a gracious hostess, but she knew that no minister's wife was expected to voice an opinion on any policy decision. Hers was a silent role. In relation to her husband and the church, she was to be cheerful, courteous, agreeable, but above all, supportive and silent.

She had a soft laugh that seemed to bubble from inside when the family and one or two of the children's friends went for fishing and camping trips in the hills outside of town. Mrs. Shaw laughed often on these excursions and would hug the children and say, "Isn't God good?" Life, I suppose, and its pleasures were simple for her. She saw no more than a couple of movies in her life, and a trip to Buffalo to visit a sister was the farthest she ever went from her western Pennsylvania home.

Her appearance was as simple as her life. She wore her hair in a bun which rested at the nape of her neck. The style never changed. Partly because it was easy to fix. But partly, too, because it was an indeterminate fashion—neither too fancy nor lacking in neatness. This was her constant style— never chic, but not dowdy either. She must never outdo the most fashionable woman in the congregation, but she must be better dressed than the poorest, lest the community think the church did not provide adequately for its pastor.

Not that her only abilities had to do with homemaking—she was remarkable in other ways. Her voice was strong and never off-key. She played the piano with ease and a sure touch. She joked that every theological student looked, before he proposed, for a girl who could play the piano and sing. It was from this combination of talents that she received her greatest recognition.

Reverend Shaw was spread a bit thin through all his ministry, with three to five churches under his direction. Sunday was church day for his family. The boys always sat with one of the men from the congregation—in recognition, I suppose, of the fact that the firm masculine hand which usually held them in check was at that point otherwise engaged. Mrs. Shaw looked after the three girls in the same seat each Sunday. I remember no scenes or scandals occasioned by their conduct.

When, because of his itineration, the pastor might be late for worship or for prayer meeting, Mrs. Shaw would begin the service. In this role, she was the agent of her husband and as such was fully acceptable as a leader. Her responsibilities as a sort of assistant pastor were unanimously accepted as a part of a hidden contract. She was often the first person to call on a new family in town with a warm and welcoming smile, a bunch of flowers, a jar of jelly, or a freshly baked loaf, along with an invitation to Sunday worship and an outline of church school classes available to any offspring of the new residents.

Most times she visited a bereaved family before the undertaker had appeared and stayed to do whatever was needed. For weddings she usually provided the wedding march and on many nights was a witness for an eloping couple who wanted to be "hitched."

As I put it down now, it seems a limited and limiting life. Surely it was circumscribed by the expectations of a clergyman husband, a congregation that had very definite ideas about how she should live, and her own perceptions of her role. To be Mrs. Shaw was for her a "calling," as definite as that of her husband. She was a part of the ministry of Christ in the world—and if it seemed a small world, a limited world, so be it, for this was God's will for her.

The annual meeting of the conference was a time eagerly anticipated. There she heard of another, larger world where the Lord and the church she served were important too. It was a time of stimulation, education, and direction. But it was a time of pleasure as well, where she saw again old friends and shared professional stories and jokes with others like herself who shared with husbands in "partnership for the Lord."

It was from Mrs. Shaw's son that I learned about the source of the serenity and grace with which she met life. He said: "As a boy growing up in parsonages with cracker-box rooms and thin walls, I could hear my mother's prayers. There were always expressions of gratitude for food and shelter, for love and caring, for me and my brother and sisters. Often she asked for guidance in dealing with some misdemeanor we had committed, but always pleading for protection for us through childhood and youth; for my father and his ministry; for the church and its people; and for herself, God love her, that she might have understanding and a Christian spirit."

During World War II that same son, severely wounded, lay on the battlefield for hours before the medics could evacuate him. Through that time of darkness and pain, he remembered his mother and her prayers. He knew that she was probably praying for him even then, so he hung on.

That was her life—passive, accepting, supporting, and filled with love for her fellow beings and for God.

CAROL THE CAMPUS QUEEN

She was my college friend, and a more unlikely prospect to be the "Mistress of the Manse" I couldn't imagine. In our junior year she had been selected May Queen, and there was no doubt about it, she was a smashing beauty. Her eyes were blue and merry, perfect companions for a mouth just ready to burst into laughter, which it often did, even at her own expense. She was always ready for mischief and worried not too much about rules. I remember the time she got caught letting a couple of sorority sisters in the fire-escape door because they had overstayed the sign-in time. She escaped with a lecture from the housemother which she would imitate to perfection, sending all of us into gales of laughter.

She didn't really take things seriously, not even her studies, though she never failed any of them. From my viewpoint she was a free, irrepressible spirit with a great lust for living. And the fellows followed her in packs. She never settled for one, as so many of us did; still she had a date for every campus event.

Like every generation, we believed that we lived in the worst of times. Dark clouds were gathering over Europe as Adolf Hitler gobbled up more and more territory and the Old World streets echoed to the tramp of storm-trooper boots.

The draft was reactivated and we all grumbled, but we never thought of disobeying its requirements. It was the law and we would obey. Consequently, male students would receive their "greetings" from the President and leave school to report for induction. It was an unsettled time for all of us, yet campus life continued on.

One weekend, a sorority sister of ours had promised her fiancé, a seminarian, to get a date for his friend. She asked Carol, who treated it as a joke. "A theological student! Me?" she said, and laughed uproariously. "But then I've never tried it before, so why not?"

When Carol returned to the dorm that evening she was unusually quiet, with a glow about her I'd never seen before. Suddenly Carol was turning down dates on campus and waiting by the phone for calls which came frequently. She began to live for the weekends when Jim would arrive on campus, and they would spend hours in a remote corner of the library or the lounge in deep conversation.

On a spring morning, sprawled on the beds in my room, Carol and I had a talk. "I'm in love, you know," she said. "And it isn't at all the way I would have planned it. Isn't it a joke that I had to fall for someone studying to be a preacher? But it's happened. I'm completely gone on the guy. The miracle of it is that he loves me, too. We can have a beautiful and good life together. After all, I'll be marrying Jim, not a minister."

And so she did, on a soft summer day with sunshine and flowers and the laughter of happiness shared with friends. I preceded her down the aisle as a bridesmaid and I saw the look on Jim's face as he waited at the altar. There was no doubt that he loved her, but the profession he had chosen would always come first. I knew that if accommodation had to be made, Carol would have to be the one to change. I truly hoped it wouldn't mean the loss of the merry, fun-loving girl who was my friend.

We were engulfed by war only five months later and life changed for us all. Jim and Carol were in a small, suburban church outside Philadelphia. The male population disappeared into the Army or spent ten- to twelve-hour shifts in defense industries, where they were joined by a great many women who exchanged their aprons for a riveting gun and found a new sense of independence and freedom.

Carol found herself assuming duties she had not dreamed would be a part of her new life. She learned cheerfully to share Jim's time and concern with other families, especially when the dreaded news of death or injury was delivered. She accepted the fact that she, without jealousy, had to allow Jim to be a source of comfort and strength to other women, often when she herself was tired or lonely or frightened too. She discovered a great deal about the people with whom she lived, but even more about herself.

When the war ended, Carol and her husband moved to a larger church in a medium-sized city. Their family now included two beautiful children. With the return of the men from distant battlefields, the tempo of church life increased. Carol complained, but not bitterly, of how she was caring for the children virtually alone.

"Jim is never home," she said. "There is always a meeting of one sort or another that he has to attend, or services to be conducted, or people to see, or paper work to do. But if I grouse about it, it is almost as though I'm rebelling against God. After all, isn't Jim his agent?"

I did not remind her of her earlier words. She had learned that to be married to Jim was to be married to a minister; the man and his calling were not separate but one and the same.

Coping with the realities of life under the stress of wartime and understanding a role dictated both by the man she married and by the people to whom he ministered had sobered Carol and matured her. Life no longer seemed a lark to her but it was still an adventure.

She was a catalyst for many of Jim's plans and programs. He looked to her for support, not only as a participant but

as an emotional prop as well. She was his sounding board as
well as his critic. All the while she cared for the children,
cleaned the house, cooked the meals, and nursed the children
through colds, measles, and chicken pox. She often found
herself wearied by both the home front and the church front.

She realized, as she had not before her wedding, that
people saw her contributions as wife, mother, and church-
woman as filling an expected and accepted assignment. She
was, in a sense, taken for granted, an extension of her husband and his ministry. At the time she did not question the
philosophy, for the busy life didn't leave time for loneliness
or longing.

Carol had become a "typical minister's wife," though she
would have been infuriated by the phrase.

"I'm not gloomy and pious, and I'm still myself—whatever that may be. I'm trying to find answers to questions I
haven't asked yet. But I do know this: I'm more than simply
someone's mother or wife. I realize there is a big world where
I may make a difference." She had developed an inner quality
and had become a caring, creative, and, yes, supportive person. She had found in her life of service to God and to Jim
that she could tap the roots of that earlier zest for life. I
hadn't lost my college friend. She was still there, but other
layers of being had been added.

PROFESSIONALLY TRAINED BETTY

We talked often over a cup of coffee after meetings of a
committee for fair housing. She wasn't pretty but she had an
interesting, intelligent face and a certain individual style
(which would team a worn, hand-knit sweater with well-
tailored slacks of an obviously quality tweed, and this at a

time when slacks were not a fashion "must"). We discussed
the cause in which we were both involved and then moved
on to the more personal aspects of our lives. "I seldom volunteer the fact that I'm married to a clergyman," she once said,
"because that seems to make me suspect on both sides of the
spectrum. On the one hand, I'm regarded as a do-gooder,
possessing more sentiment than skill, and as a manipulated
revolutionary on the other."

As our relationship grew, I learned a great deal more
about Betty that illuminated this remark. The climate of the
time was stormy; issues were explored in an aura of heated
controversy that forced one to take sides. It was away from
the conflict, in a quieter, more contemplative mood, that
Betty was willing to reveal some of the facets of her life.

She met her husband on the seminary campus and they
courted amid the stimulation of intellectual learning and
stretching. As a young person, she had been deeply involved
in her church; the church school curriculum and the youth
programs had made her aware of a further dimension of the
church's mission—the advocacy role for the weak and disad-
vantaged in society. So, she had chosen a college major in
social work and beyond that the seminary campus, with no
clear idea of where it was all leading. Meeting Bill settled that
question in part. They were married and he became pastor
in a medium-sized town with the usual number of social
problems.

They had decided to plan a family when they both felt
ready for the responsibility, and when time and money factors seemed auspicious. That decision freed Betty to plunge
into the life of the parish and the community, which she did
with gusto.

She was asked to plan programs for the women of the local
church and for the larger judiciary to which it belonged. In
the beginning her ideas were received, if not warmly, at least

as a part of a newer thrust claiming the attention of women everywhere. No one felt called to question her sincerity or her information, but she recognized in an intuitive way that some of the women were uncertain about her judgment. When she planned a unit on poverty for the circle meetings, it was obvious that the ladies tolerated the subject but there was no real demand for further exploration or, more importantly, action.

She had a sense of failure and rejection. She became a volunteer in community agencies that welcomed her participation and leadership. More and more time and effort were spent outside the program of the church. "I find my involvement personally satisfying," she said, "but I have to be so careful that I don't get the kind of publicity that links Bill with my activity. There are people who would make it uncomfortable for him because of me." She tried to make her contribution in a subtle manner without compromising her convictions. She found it difficult at best, impossible and frustrating at worst.

One day she told me she was going to take a job that had been offered to her with a community agency. "I'm tired of doing for nothing what I've been trained to do, and which I see other people being paid to do. Sometimes, in my moments of depression, I feel used by the church, by the agencies, by other people, and I get resentful."

I knew what she meant. Women were joining the employed ranks in ever larger numbers. The culture was increasingly suggesting that women would find fulfillment and freedom through a paycheck. At the same time, all types of service agencies were demanding more volunteers to staff their programs. Many women facing the dilemma were opting for jobs and the salaries that went with them.

With her free time and energy limited by the demands of a newly launched career, Betty became less and less a part of the church organization, especially of the women. She still recognized that the church and her faith were the wellsprings of her motivation and the real focus of her life.

"I don't know what I'm going to be," she observed one day, "much less what my role as a pastor's wife will become. But I do know it is going to be quite different from what it was before."

The role of the clergy wife has changed in the decades represented by these profiles. That change has affected the ministry of the church and the structure of the clergy family relationship, bringing both satisfaction and frustration. The information from the Task Force research plus my own observations and experience as a clergy wife will inform our examination of the wife of the present day.

Chapter II

Neither Clergy nor Laity

He was an ordinary-looking man with sandy hair, ruddy skin, and of middle age. His words were a reflection of an ordinary attitude. "I can't understand what she wants," he said. "Isn't it enough being my wife and the mother of our children?" He had not once mentioned her name or given any idea of her personality, her abilities, or even her appearance. He had failed, in fact, to present her as a person at all. That was the key to the whole problem. He could very well be a sort of "Everyman," and it is against the very image he described that women have been struggling.

After World War II, with a newly roused sense of independence, women found themselves involved in the suburban "togetherness" of new communities, new houses, and growing families. They became part of an attempt to confer on suburban motherhood something of the esteem and value that the women of pioneer generations had enjoyed. It was a somewhat short-lived endeavor because the social scientists, in looking at American youth, began to deride what was termed "momism," and demographers, in looking at the world, began to cry out against the "population explosion." With their relationship to childbearing and nurture, these problems aroused in women a new sense of guilt and purpose-

lessness that added a further dimension to the feminist movement. It was a deeper dimension than the push for equality.
It centered on a search for identity, which the dictionary
defines as being a specific person or as the distinctive character belonging to an individual. It was and is, in essence, a
desire to have a meaningful understanding and love of self
that brings dignity and satisfaction to woman's role in contemporary society. With an increasingly higher level of education, American woman began to wish to be herself, to
choose what to be, and to determine her own reality free of
past imposed definitions. It has been an arduous search filled
with pitfalls.

Early on, the perception was gained that the identity of
women has been determined by others: fathers, husbands,
even children. The great majority of women had accepted
men's definitions and had obeyed the seemingly natural order
of things. For a long time that order had implied that women
are to be valued, not as persons with individual and distinctive skills, interests, and possibilities, but as supportive beings
to the structures built by men.

Those structures had undergone tremendous change in
the marketplace and in the home. Once a filler of needs,
restricted to the traditional triangle of *Kinder, Küche, Kirche*
(children, kitchen, church), women in a technological, urban,
and industrialized setting found they were consigned to the
primary role of consumers. They were to be buyers and users
of all the gadgets, garments, and groceries that industry, led
by men, produced. This was, in fact, a restatement of an
eighteenth- and nineteenth-century social designation of the
coddled female, whether wife or daughter, as valuable evidence of the wealth of her husband or father.

Freud had declared that anatomy is destiny and, thus,
reinforced the status quo. The modern view recognized that
differences between men and women exist but that those

differences are no indication of superiority of one over the other, or of the right of one to define nature and duty for the other. Increasingly, women began to understand and reach for a destiny that is broader and more difficult than anatomy —and more promising. They long for a definition of woman developed by what she is and not by what she does.

In addition to the assigned role of support, women were to fulfill a private role. The male traditionally has been the public figure, involved in the arena of significant events where laws are made, contracts negotiated, and the tide of human endeavor determined. In the private domain which was women's place, because of the limited and limiting identity given them, women had an inner sense of becoming "dodo birds." Since there were no requirements for the job, they could literally block out self-realization and the development of potential. A cartoon, which pictures a man and a woman at a party sitting together in the midst of a crowd, vividly depicts this conception. The man is saying to his companion: "You're stupid. I like that in a woman."

More and more women, aware of the currents of social change, their view broadened beyond the home by better education, their perceptions heightened by the pressures for equality and justice, their concepts of possibilities deepened as they found new understanding of frustrations, became a part of an idea whose time had come.

It is not news that the church is challenged by these currents of social change which intimately affect women. By its very nature, the church is affected more profoundly than other institutions. Its roots in the Jewish tradition were heavily masculine with patriarchy established as policy. By the time of Christ and the New Testament the status of women had become far more restricted and their role far more subordinate than previously. The true spirit of the tradition is revealed in the prayer that men recited daily in the synagogue: "Blessed art Thou, O Lord . . . for not making me a woman." (Significantly this prayer is no longer offered as a part of Jewish ritual, having been changed in recent years to reflect new insights.) With the emergence of Christianity, the complex history of women's role in our society began. On the face of it, Christianity raised the level of womankind. Paul's assertion that "there is neither Jew nor Greek, there is neither slave nor free, there is neither male nor female, for you are all one in Jesus Christ" (Gal. 3:28) was an enunciation of equality between the sexes which had never before been present in human society.

Unfortunately, for generations Biblical interpretation was permeated with a sense of male superiority and a sense of the female as a secondary being. The fact that God was and is presented as a male is the ultimate expression of such beliefs which were used to strengthen the status quo, to discourage change, and to allow the church to mirror the society rather than to redeem it.

In more modern times the view regarding women as subordinate was even built into ecclesiastical structures. Here, too, women were to be supporters of the organizations built by men. They were encouraged to contribute through mite and missionary societies and ladies aid groups to the mission of the church which was planned, organized, and administered by male bureaucracies. Furthermore, theirs was a private role, for any share in policymaking was denied them under Biblical injunction as traditionally interpreted.

It is true, however, that the church was seeking to respond to these feminist winds of change. More and more denominations were endorsing the ordination of women as clergy and as officers and leaders in the congregation. It was a slow process and as the tempo of change accelerated so did the pressure for full participation by women in the church. The church, through its educational programs and its women's organizations, was emphasizing the cry for justice and equality by minorities and by women. Women's groups, carrying on a role as educator and informer, using study materials often developed by women, included not only the missionary aspect of the church's life but the examination of social issues as well. In many ways they were responsible for arousing the conscience of the church to a new awareness for concern and action. A trend developed at that time which is affecting the present day. Young women began resisting the traditional organizational forms of women's programs in the church. They were not willing to invest their time, often limited, in traditional women's groups which they perceived as ineffective and unimportant. They were beginning to look for a more aggressive and public role and they were finding it in other kinds of groups—such as the League of Women Voters, Women in Community Service, and a variety of civil rights and social action agencies. Gradually, in many areas, the women's association assumed a lesser role than it had played in the past.

Slowly the movement within the church began to take form and focus. It no longer addressed itself simply to isolated examples of attitude and discrimination within the body but turned to the broader issue of recognition of women as human beings. For centuries the message of the church had declared that we are all, both men and women, created by God as unique persons with differing gifts and vocations but united in a common humanity. The church found itself challenged to make its message a reality as it pursued its ministry. Theologians began seriously to examine the exegesis of Scripture and to discover new insight into truths that had always been there. Women's concerns began to be treated seriously and women's abilities recognized and accepted.

In the milieu of church and society the clergy wife finds herself searching for her identity even as other women. She is affected by the forces that beset others, but her attempt to find herself and her gifts, to define and develop her place, is pursued through a maze of perceptions that have little relation to the rest of womankind. She is in many ways a captive of a role that has its roots in the past, since stereotypes never change as fast as do social realities. For too long the minister's wife has been confined to a kind of religious ghetto by her role both in the church and in society. She is forced to decide whether to renounce her own uniqueness and her own selfhood by conforming to the image of a model minister's wife, or whether to resist and thus maintain the inner core of individuality and freedom that makes her different from all others. She is pressured to conform both to a male definition of her place and to an institutional one as well.

WHAT CHURCH MEMBERS EXPECT

No doubt the institutional role of a clergy wife is defined, at least in part, by the congregation. In order to develop some understanding of the perceptions of the minister's wife that are held by lay persons, a questionnaire was prepared and distributed to a random sampling of the laity. An interesting profile emerges from those questionnaires returned which, if typical, provide other information about the church as well. The age distribution of the replies consisted overwhelmingly of those between fifty and sixty-nine years of age—some 67 percent of the total—while only 22 percent were between twenty and forty-nine years of age. The respondents were 77 percent female and most likely to live in a suburban community or a small town as contrasted with a fully rural or an urban setting. Their educational level indicated that 24 percent were high school graduates, 15 percent had some college education, with 29 percent having finished college and received degrees, 8 percent had some form of technical training, and 23 percent had received postgraduate-level education. Their careers were varied; 39 percent were homemakers and 17 percent were teachers—the largest groupings. The next largest included the retirees, secretaries, and social workers. The balance were involved in such divergent occupations as physicians and farmers, engineers and factory workers, salespersons and librarians, nurses and directors of Christian education, accountants, and one research editor. The great majority of those responding were involved in a leadership responsibility in the local congregation. Only 11 percent categorized themselves as members only, holding no specific office.

How well the lay person knows the clergy wife does not seem to affect willingness to define her role. The middle answer of "Fairly well" was selected by 60 percent to describe their knowledge of their own minister's wife. A larger proportion of the remainder stated that they had a speaking acquaintance with her than answered that they knew her well.

What did these respondents expect of the minister's wife? The foremost requirement was that she be a participant in the life of the congregation. Several even said that she should be an *enthusiastic* participant, though some others limited this congregational activity by saying, "No more than any other church member." In addition, she should be supportive of her husband, reflect his work in home and family life, express love and concern for people. In lesser degree she should trust God, share in the women's work and program, be a dedicated Christian, be a leader in the congregation—as she wishes— be a good hostess, and be her husband's intellectual equal. The interesting facet of this data is that 15 percent declared that she should be free to be herself and 4 percent more suggested that she should make up her own mind about attending church and sharing her husband's attitudes.

As one examines this list of qualities and expectations there seems little change from expressions of the past. It is, in a sense, an awesome list. The evidence is indicative that the clergy wife is still largely viewed from an institutional perspective. But the replies indicated a small though basic change. There are some expressions that recognize her as an individual. One answer stated:

> "This past year she has had a part-time job! I am *glad* that she feels free to satisfy her own needs this way. . . . I think the day has passed when a minister's wife has to do nothing or do only 'church' things."

Another recognized the fact that some women wish to define their role in terms of their husband's ministry, and this was viewed as an individual and person-centered matter. The statement said:

> "If she wants to participate and be active and be an extension of her husband (two full-time workers for the price of one), it should be her choice."

In my own experience there are several areas of expectation that have not yet been expressed. Often the minister's wife is viewed as a paraprofessional with specialized knowledge. She is called upon to be a resource person in a variety of fields. She is expected to be fully aware of the program and ecclesiastical structure of the denomination beyond the local congregation. She is often asked to provide information about content and availability of a number of materials within the life of the church. She is expected to provide Biblical and theological insights beyond those of the ordinary church member, and is called upon to counsel for a number of spiritual and personal problems. Such expectations can be a positive force for her own growth and maturity if she accepts the challenge and becomes informed about as many aspects of current program and Biblical thought as possible. There is, however, a current phenomenon that is causing personal conflict as it relates to her own paraprofessionalism. As more and more women have entered seminary and have emerged to be ordained as ministers, their fully professional status can become a threat to the validity of the role of the clergy wife, already threatened by social change. The status of the clergy wife is bound to be affected in the perception of lay persons as they come to know a greater number of female ministers in their professional role.

An illustration of this possibility was given to me by the wife of an East Coast pastor in a sophisticated, suburban church.

"When we first went to the congregation several years ago I was called upon by the women to assist with program planning and leadership development. I was qualified because of past involvement and I truly enjoyed it and wanted to do it. When a new staff member came whose wife had attended seminary, she was *hired* to do the very same thing I was doing as an unpaid volunteer."

A meeting of a church committee or a phone call from a parishioner illustrates another expectation of the laity in which the wife speaks for her husband. "What will your husband think of that, Mrs. Jones?" or "Will that be acceptable to the pastor, Mrs. Jones?" are typical questions. Sometimes planning comes to a halt because an authoritative word is required and the pastor is considered able to give it *in absentia* through his wife. This views the clergy wife as an extension of her husband. Some aspects of this surfaced in the lay responses. It is an impersonalized role which confines the clergy wife to being a ventriloquist's dummy of sorts.

Related to this view, surely, is the penchant of the laity for introducing the clergy spouse as "This is our minister's wife." Wives at workshops, in conversation, and in responses to the questionnaire have indicated this as a particular sore spot for them. While indicating her frustrations, one said, "I am seen, introduced, and greeted as 'The Minister's Wife,' not Jane Doe, social worker, intelligent and capable person." Usually, the laity sees this practice as an attempt to indicate a measure of respect, pride, and love for their minister's wife. For the clergy wife, however, in the light of her self-identity, which is conditioned by today's climate for recognition as a person in one's own right, it has become symbolic of her assignment to a role in which she is dehumanized and denied acknowledgment of her own uniqueness. It is significant of a healthy change that opportunity to express these feelings in dialogue is being provided by the church.

As the clergy wife is expected to be an extension of her husband, she is also delegated to represent the church. Often her interests, abilities, skills, and even her appearance, are judged and accepted on the basis of the congregational image of itself. In other words, a conservative membership would expect the minister's wife to reflect those ideas and relationships which augment its view of ministry. In a similar way, a liberal and socially active group would not welcome her participation in a theologically fundamental or politically conservative activity. I suppose, in a sense, they see her as an extension not only of her husband but also of themselves. This is a dangerous statement to make, since it is capable of being misunderstood—there are so many individual variables in a local congregation. It is true, however, that churches tend to develop a particular orientation that is reflective of the majority. It is quite difficult for the clergy wife to maintain her own personal direction if it is not a part of the climate of the congregation. Often in the judicatory and denominational realms and in the area of community life, both ecumenical and secular, she is considered a representative of her church. This makes it difficult for her to share her skills and abilities as her own individual gifts—they are too often perceived as a part of a taken-for-granted institutional response. Though this may happen to some lay leaders, it seems to be more or less a general rule for the clergy wife.

A final observation in regard to lay perception of the clergy wife: In actual practice she is regarded as different—not professional, as is the clergy, and not fully laity, either—she has her own special place. That place holds a certain fascination, significance, and mystery about it which affects her relationships. Many lay persons expressed the fact that they expect their minister's wife to be warm, loving, and concerned for people and to be their friend but gave no indication of their own responsibility in this regard. It appears that they desire to be included in her world but do not see the need to reciprocate.

WHAT HER MATE EXPECTS

Every girl arrives at the altar with stars in her eyes, and a mental image of the life she will lead with the groom who awaits her. He too has expectations of the woman who promises to be his wife. This joint definition is important for every married woman. It establishes her place in her husband's life, defines the perimeter of her activity, determines in large measure their relationship, and decides the degree of involvement in his work. For the clergyman, this perception of roles is a part of basic commitment to the marriage bond. Twenty or thirty years ago a small proportion of seminarians were married while they were still in school. As a result, they had some measure of the kinds of qualities they expected to find before they said "I do." Often these assumptions were based on a strongly idealized, overly demanding tradition that led to frustration and conflict for the wife.

Today the trend is to marry before entering seminary, and so the expectation for the wife, as she relates to her husband's vocation, is somewhat fuzzy, opening the way to unexpected and uncommunicated demands. For the woman, this is particularly traumatic if her self-expectation differs greatly from that which is imposed on her. The two most important components of this imposition are undoubtedly her husband and his congregation. The greatest of these is, in all probability, her husband. Much depends on the sort of man he happens to be. Most of the time, even for those who entered the profession after pursuing another career, he tends to feel his work and the church are of primary importance to him. Every clergy wife, at some time in her marriage, has had to come to terms with a possessive rival in the form of her husband's work and she knows that she rarely can win in a confrontation with this competitor. This would indicate, then, in a very real sense that the clergy wife is perceived and relegated to a secondary priority by her husband. This realization is shattering to female pride and self-image and places tremendous pressure upon the wife to reconcile her romantic ideals with reality. Other wives whose husbands' occupations are different may experience this same trauma but they can object. By the very nature of his calling, the minister engages in "holy" work; if the wife asks for different priorities, she is, in essence, questioning God.

Not long ago a young family man who for a number of

years has felt a calling to the ministry began actively to consider entering seminary though successfully engaged in a career of public service. His wife does not share his feeling and is quite open about her opposition. She states that she has no sense of call to become a minister's wife, that she feels ill equipped and is unwilling to make the sacrifices she perceives as necessary for such a change. Furthermore, she did not marry a minister in the first place. Her husband, apparently, does not hear her and continues to plan what is, to him, a valid option. While extreme, I believe his attitude illustrates the perception of a great many clergymen. Their call to the ministry is the greatest reality for them. The thoughts and feelings of their wives have no substance as they relate to this central fact of their lives. Their call to the ministry tends to be total and all-involving.

The overriding expectation of the clergy for their wives (one shared by the laity) is that she be supportive. Responses from 122 clergymen indicate this fact as they define the role of their spouses. This support takes different forms. The first of these is physical and deals with homemaking and family care. The wife is to assume major responsibility for a cheerful, comfortable, clean house and happy, well-adjusted children. In many ways, this does not differ markedly from the role of other wives. For her, however, it often involves little raw material in the form of money or housing and thus demands extra ingenuity, creativity, and acceptance.

Closely related is the second support which is emotional. It is to their wives that ministers turn for a catharsis of resentment, disappointment, and hurt, making their wives combination confessors and wailing walls. Such support is obviously to be accessible, nonjudgmental, and very partisan. Many times this assignment leads to strain and difficulty for the wife in her relationship with persons in the congregation or community. She must silently bury the knowledge of some individual's effect upon her husband's being and work. In some ways she is, in her husband's eyes, a burden bearer upon whom he can load all the baggage that accumulates as he relates to those in the congregation.

Programmatic support is the third support system the clergy wife provides for her husband. Today's church life is extremely complex with all types of administrative, educational, financial, and social action responsibilities delegated to the pastor. Usually he relies upon his wife to become a partner in at least one area of the church's program. Sometimes it is with music or in Christian education that she makes her contribution. There have even been cases where the minister counted upon his wife's secretarial skills to augment his limited administrative abilities. A large proportion of ministers depend upon their wives to be involved with the women's work to relieve them of the need to understand or relate to this aspect of the church life. Most of the time she is free to select her own area of concentration. Increasingly, particularly among younger clergy, the wife is being freed to elect for noninvolvement with any program thrust, if this is her desire.

Indications are that the clergyman takes seriously the marital injunction that "they shall be one flesh." He tends to look upon his wife as an extension of himself, much as the laity do. He expects her to report reactions of various kinds to him on matters ranging from sermons to church finances and depends upon her for complete loyalty. One of his fears is that conflict between them on any issue might become public. Her union with him is to be so complete that it cannot allow any differences to be seen by the congregation. The new asserting of self by women generally, and the clergy wife particularly, has resulted in a new awareness on the part of husbands. The change has made him more available for dis-

cussion, even argument, and has developed a greater willingness to listen. Certainly, a new climate of openness will allow
both minister and wife a more human and liberated approach
to their marriage and to the congregational life in which they
are key participants.

A significant number of responses indicated that the conviction is held that a wife be "free to be herself." The space
allotted for answers did not permit a lengthy exposition of
what this would involve either in freedom or in identity. The
fact remains that women need great motivation, support, and
encouragement from the most important male in their lives,
their husbands, to break out of stereotype images and live
their lives to the full as human beings. This is doubly true for
clergy wives!

WHAT SHE EXPECTS OF HERSELF

A significant scene is portrayed in the fictional story of a
minister's wife entitled *Papa's Wife* by Thyra Ferré Bjorn. In
it the main character has just learned that she is to become
a grandmother and she says, "Now I will be Grandma Fron-
zak instead of Papa's wife." Those few words express the
lives of so many women, their identity, especially in their own
minds, defined by others. Evidence gathered from the responses of 315 clergy wives reveals that there are three major
ways in which they attempt to deal with their perceptions of
role definition. They are:

1. To conform to the traditional role expectations of
   serving and supporting;
2. To revolt and become completely uninvolved in
   any way as a clergy wife;

3. To homogenize the realities and expectations of her life with her own needs and aspirations.

As one examines the root meaning of the word "stereotype" the discovery is made that it has its origin in the realm of printing. It refers to a plate case in metal that will reproduce its form on raw material pressed against its surface. In conforming to the limits imposed by an unchanging, developed definition, a woman must become role-centered. She learns the perimeters of allowable activity and restricts her life to them. Like the raw material, she allows the type plate —a hodgepodge of perceptions—to press her life and mold her being into a form alien, perhaps, to her real self. Usually the process of self-discovery is painful and slow, so it is much simpler to fit into the ruts carved out by others. This involves a withdrawal from reality. It is a moving away from people. Younger wives, especially, indicate that they reject this manner of coping.

Like a pendulum, moving from one extreme to the other, the reaction by many who reject the traditional role is to revolt against any definition at all. Unfortunately, this approach is also role-centered, placing emphasis upon negative response and seeking identity away from the role. It is a moving against people. In the search for self these clergy wives try to escape from all that they perceive as limiting or phony. In their struggle to be self-directed they stand outside the church in a self-conscious and often self-centered search for being.

I remember when homogenized milk appeared on the market. My children were small, and previously I had had to carefully pour the cream from the top of the bottle before they could drink the milk. When the new process was introduced, the entire contents of the bottle was permeated with the flavor and the richness of the cream in tolerable amounts.

It would appear that the majority of clergy wives are seeking to homogenize their role and permeate it with the best of the past and legitimate contributions from others. For them to find meaning and fulfillment they have to allow their own being to be a part of the total definition of their role. This means that the congregation and the husband must accept the clergy wife as an individual and permit her to find her own particular place in the life of the church and community. In this way, the minister's wife has the glorious freedom to *give* of herself rather than being required to fulfill the expectations of others. Such action is not without risk. If the clergy wife is open, she is vulnerable to hurt and misunderstanding. If she gives, she is open to rejection. The questionnaires reveal that rejection is not an uncommon occurrence. One definition articulated by a minister's wife says it very well:

"I think my role as a minister's wife has dramatically changed, because I have changed. It's been a hard and painful road. No one, six years ago in seminary, could have prepared me for this, except personal growth or development groups. But, had they been available, I'm not sure I would have gone, since I was so positive I knew it all.

"I'm very happy here and most of all I'm very happy with myself. I'm still discovering who I am and that is very exciting to me. For the first time, I have friends in the church who really care and are supportive and with whom I have risked myself and my needs. And for the first time I'm able to meet their needs, too.

"My 'role' is what I make it, in terms of myself, my Christian and personal growth needs, and my need to give in a Christian community. Above all, my 'role' is not a role. It is authentic and real, and comes from within."

THE SAME BUT DIFFERENT

Again and again on all three classifications of response, the statement was made that the minister's wife is no different from any other member of the church. Yet evidence would seem to indicate that she is in reality not regarded as a fully participating member of the church on an equal level with other persons of the congregation. A minute percentage of the clergy wives indicate election to office, and 40 percent of the laity and 51 percent of the clergy voice opposition to her participation in the decision-making bodies. This would strongly indicate that the clergy wife occupies a "super feminine" role in the congregation—supportive and serving, yes; planning and deciding, no! In the climate of today's society where the ideal of participatory democracy is a part of most organizations, this lack of freedom for the clergy wife to express or mold opinion is clearly out of step with the times. The wives recognize their status—and in many ways resent their disenfranchisement and their lack of freedom to participate fully.

This denial is based on a variety of assumptions and an assortment of unspoken rules that govern political life in the church. It is this silent quality which adds to their repressive nature. In a broad way, these assumptions can be grouped in three categories:

1. The conspiracy theory implies that the minister would be involved in a course of action, hidden and secret, through which he could achieve some unidentified end. Naturally if his wife were an officer, she would support and be a part of the conspiracy.
2. The power bloc process is an intimation that there is a move by the clergyman to wrest power from

      delegated authority for his own ungoverned con-
      trol. Again, his wife would be a tool in such a ploy.

3.   The manipulative method assumes that the minis-
      ter would try shrewdly to manage the ruling body
      so that he can achieve his own selfish and possibly
      even corrupt purposes. As a member of the official
      group, his wife would willingly abet such devious
      control.

When clothed in such language, these implications seem
ludicrous, but they are a part of the agenda of every congregation to a greater or lesser degree. They often determine
who is elected to office and the development of principles that
ascertain how it is done. It might easily be asked: "What
manner of man do we perceive our pastor to be? A power-
hungry, corrupt, grasping, manipulative person, not deserv-
ing of our trust?" There is probably no one of goodwill who
would make such a charge against the pastor, nor that his
wife is such a weak, ineffective, dishonest individual that she
would allow herself to be used in such blatant ways. Further,
they do not view the marriage relationship of minister and
wife in such a cynical way. They would deny that their
judgment of their fellow members would comprehend them
as able to be moved about like pawns on a board. Yet, though
not couched in these phrases, clergy wives are denied an
opportunity by these assumptions to experience the honor
and the opportunity for recognized leadership and witness in
the congregation.

Undoubtedly, the fear of open discord with their wives
hinders some ministers from adopting a more open attitude.
There is here the hidden implication of a lack of trust in the
wife's good judgment and good manners for conduct becoming to a Christian. One minister was honest enough to say
that he was hesitant to have his wife be a part of the ruling

body where he must exercise his administrative ability, which he categorized as his weakest skill. Many clergymen will presume to answer for their wives and declare that they have no interest in such service when, as pastors, they would never presume to answer for a member of the congregation.

Certainly, if one recognizes that clergy wives encompass a vast variety of abilities, temperaments, and desires, it is obvious that not all would wish or be suited for church office, but their disqualification on the basis of their choice of a marriage partner is surely unjust. One clergyman put it very well:

> "She is currently on the session. I feel it appropriate as an expression of her faith of which she should not be deprived just because she is my wife."

If she is denied elective office, she still finds many gaps to fill in church life. The questionnaires reveal a real relationship between the frustrations felt by clergy wives and the expectation that they perform unfilled responsibilities that are unwanted by others. This, in spite of their interest, ability, or desire to do so. Here, as in so many areas of church program, they are dependent upon "on-the-job training" to equip them for the obligations either thrust upon them or willingly accepted. In a pursuit of excellence, this surely leads to a sense of dissatisfaction and disappointment.

One expression of support for the full participation of the clergy wife in the local congregation was the adoption of a Bill of Rights for Ministers' Spouses by the General Assembly of The United Presbyterian Church in the U.S.A. meeting in 1974. It reads:

> It seems necessary to affirm and define the following rights that are due to each minister's spouse as a child of God:

1. An equal right to seek employment of his or her choice.
2. An equal right to choose church membership or non-membership.
3. An equal right and responsibility to serve the mission of the church, as a member, without obligations or privileges.
4. An equal right as a member of a congregation, to be considered for election to the session and other boards and committees.

In the mid-nineteenth century when feminism was beginning, Harriet Mill, the wife of John Stuart Mill, wrote: "We deny the right of any portion of the species to decide for another portion, or any individual for another individual, what is and what is not their 'proper sphere.' The proper sphere for all human beings is the largest and highest to which they are able to attain." The true search for self leads inevitably to a relationship with God who has created us as unique, endowed us with varieties of gifts, and revealed himself in Jesus Christ. The women who are married to ministers are above all Christians. They, like all humankind, find their highest and best selves in the presence of God.

Chapter III

Marriage Under Stress

One question discussed by young women in talk sessions is: What vocation does the ideal husband have? Always at the bottom of the list are two service professions—medicine and ministry. But a doctor is preferred by a wide margin over the clergyman. His income level is considered able to overcome most of the drawbacks connected with his profession. Time and again women declare, "I'd never want to be a minister's wife!" Yet the majority of clergymen woo and marry, just as everyone else does.

Clergy wives indicated in their questionnaire responses a strong and deep emotional tie to their husbands. Better than half—59 percent—responded in the affirmative to the question: "If you had it to do over again, would you marry a minister?" Another 25 percent answered, "Probably." Many added, "If it were the same man." One reply seems to voice the feeling of the majority:

> "The man I married is still a special person—intelligent, capable, and loving."

In an age of four-letter words, the operative word for clergy wives is L-O-V-E. It leads to something they do—they marry!

As a young bride serving with my husband on the faculty of a youth conference, I was asked by the girls, "What is it like to date a minister?" as though there was some unique and mysterious quality to their dating patterns. When I shared the conversation with my husband, he laughed and said, "What do they think we are, the third sex?" There are many false images, not only about the courting customs of clergy couples but about their marriages as well. The "bridal path" is not strewn with roses and endless bliss. There is a dark side to the merger of two lives, even for clergymen.

Once, by endurance, loyalty, fear of consequences, and religious conviction, marital stress was hidden and unacknowledged. Times have changed and the enormous stresses upon the marriage tie for a clergy couple are now more openly recognized, discussed, and acted upon. Today the incidence of marital strife and divorce among the clergy has jolted the church and the public sector as well.

The pressures that lead to frustration and discord in the life of a clergy wife can be divided into four main categories: Time, Friends, Money, Housing. Although stress related to these broad designations is not limited to the clergy marriage, their manifestation is peculiar to and aggravated by life in the ministry. Perhaps the best way to illustrate is to turn directly to the words of the clergy wives themselves.

Age 27, wife of four years:

> "My husband—'Mr. Nice Guy,' to everyone but me. Not that he isn't nice to me, but he puts everyone and everything before me and our son. There is always something that needs to be done in the church before he can help me or spend time with me.
>
> "I need time for myself—by myself. I feel shut in

with a small baby, and those needs aren't always met by my 'ever going someplace' husband.

"Maybe if you could educate our husbands to treat their wives as just members of the church, we might see them more often, and when they do, it might even be with a cheerful heart!"

Age 30, married for seven years:

"My primary concern is that my husband and I have time daily to grow as a couple. I certainly do not mind spending several nights each week alone and doing some things alone that I would prefer doing with him, but we still need *some* time together."

Age 35, married for fifteen years:

"As I get older, I feel we do not allow enough time to be ourselves and do things alone. I almost feel as if I'm lonely for companionship. I hate to be always almost demanding it."

Age 60, married for thirty-nine years:

"How I have always wished I could have personal friends without creating jealousy. I do realize, though, that this is partly my husband's choice, for he does not enjoy 'friends' as I do."

Age 34, married for twelve years, six months as clergy wife:

"A tremendous need to talk to someone outside this church and small town because everything I say and do here affects in some way my husband's ministry, and such pressure is stifling! We *both* need an opportunity to develop friendships outside this church and community."

Age 36, married for thirteen years:

"We have very little social life because ministers don't tend to get invitations to parties in small towns."

Age 63, married for thirty-seven years:

"Only for the past few years have we been financially solvent. I wish we could have purchased a home early in our ministry to have equity in retirement. Financial security is my greatest concern."

Age 32, married for nine years, five as clergy wife:

"Our low income has caused me to go back to school and then to work while our children are still young."

Age 28, married for eight years, four as clergy wife:

"Living in a manse which does not belong to us— improvements are not self-determined or on my priority."

Age 48, married for twenty-two years:

"Living in a house that is not maintained properly— ceiling in kitchen has been falling down for years, windows crumbling, hole in bathroom tile covered with plastic bag."

Age 55, married for twenty-seven years:

> "It was frustrating living in a manse and not able to
> discuss how I felt about some of the physical properties
> of it because it belonged to the church. I never felt at
> liberty to talk about my feelings."

Age 28, married for four years, three as clergy wife:

> "Trying to find a time when I can expect my husband
> to stay home and do things around the house without
> its interfering with his work or his rest."

THE CHURCH AS RIVAL

A third party is often blamed for difficulty in the marriage
relationship—another woman, another man, or parents-in-
law. The ever-present "third party" for the clergy couple is
the institution and the often insatiable demands that its members make upon the time, the energy, and the emotional
resources of the minister. Realistically, the wife is involved
in competition with the church for her husband. One wife felt
that her personal concern and need was to learn how to
handle anger toward an institution. Often the temptation is
to channel that resentment toward the institutional representative—in this case, the minister. For the clergy wife, this
involves a very private and emotional struggle that strains the
marriage even more.

One goal of the feminist movement has been to free persons to become more human and thus, with honesty, to face
their strengths and weaknesses, successes and failures. The
clergyman must do battle with two stereotypes—that of the

dominating, aggressive male and that of the confident, righteous minister of the Almighty. There are indications that many clergymen have resisted these roles in the past, and with heightened awareness more are continuing to do so.

The clergy questionnaire response to: "What do you see as your wife's greatest needs?" would indicate a recognition of the same stresses mentioned by their wives. There is, additionally, an assumption of their own responsibility to find solutions. The freedom of the wife to be an individual was the most frequent, followed by an awareness of the wife's need for her husband's time and emotional support. Living in the midst of the husband's work requires constant evaluation of the marital relationship while both are working toward a joint ministry. There is today a more common acceptance of the idea that it is not always the wife who must adjust to the parish living situation. Her husband must also be willing to compromise.

Overseas visitors to the United States observe that there is a difference between male and female friendships. As traditionally defined, they are divided by the masculine realm of "doing" and the female realm of "feeling." Consequently, the average American male is dependent upon his wife for the emotional intimacy he does not experience with his male friends. Only with his wife can he afford to express his feelings, his frustrations, and his fears. Male friendships are dominated by activity, the relationship defined by what is done together. Pride, competition, and fear deter men from seeking a trusting and intimate friendship with another male. Clergymen, by their isolated professional orientation, are even more affected.

For the clergy couple, the wife becomes the lone outlet for her husband's emotions and is in the nearly impossible position of being her husband's only "close" friend. It is a great burden for a woman to bear the pressure of being the sole object of a man's humanity. The responsibility of being all things to a man places a hardship on the love relationship of marriage. This can become stifling if one or both partners lack individual friends.

This may be one reason clergy wives express such need for close female friends. A new respect is developing for the role which talk plays in female companionship—the same talk that has been the object of jokes about kaffeeklatsches and telephone conversations. Clergy wives, denied the opportunity to share this type of friendship with women while receiving their husbands' demand for such intimacy, experience a profound sense of loneliness and depression.

The admission of such needs by clergy wives and the abandonment of a phony posture of self-sufficiency will lead to a greater maturity. The burden for initiating real friendship with the clergy wife, based on honest acceptance and appreciation, rests with the female laity.

Greater awareness of his own emotional needs by the clergyman, coupled with realistic attempts to develop the kinds of friendships that are authentic, trusting, and intimate, can alleviate this deprivation for him. By lightening the emotional burden of his wife, he will develop a stronger, more satisfying marital relationship.

MARRIAGE TO A MINISTER—NOT ALL GOOD

The Marriage Council of Philadelphia says the second highest incidence of marital problems occurs among ministers. A contributing factor may well be the fact that couples are marrying before entering seminary. Usually the wife assumes the role of breadwinner for the years of schooling. Neither these young women nor their husbands fully understand the realities of the life awaiting them in the parish. A nationwide survey reported that relatively more marital stress is experienced during the first ten years of marriage. For the clergy couple this would include the seminary years and the first critical years in the ministry.

One agency, which offers counseling, evaluation, and enrichment for clergy marriages, lists the commonest reasons given for marital difficulty. The three most frequent are:

1. The marriage partners have grown apart.
2. The wife has had it with the clergy wife role and wants a "normal" life.
3. The pastor feels his wife doesn't support him in the ministry.

These factors are not limited to young clergy couples. However, a marriage among the young is especially vulnerable. The partners are trying to firm up their external wants and needs while continuing to experience critical internal growth. After three years of educational development by the husband and a period of career experience by the wife, they find themselves with totally different needs—both expressed and unknown—as they face the parish situation. A level of maturity is an essential at this point to enable the couple to develop a marital "game plan" that is based on open and loving communication. A clear vision of priorities, both individual and joint, is also a prime ingredient.

The experience of one wife emphasizes the vital nature of these concepts for the younger clergy couples and their application to those married for a longer time.

> Immediately out of seminary, which was located in a large metropolitan area, we went to a yoked charge in a rural area. At that time, I was in great personal

conflict regarding the move, our marriage, and choosing between wife or career roles. This was a time of great stress and rebellion. As part of my own identity struggle, I refused to participate in the church programs, attempting in some way to determine and assert independence.

Having grown up in a small church, I remember constant and bitter criticisms of our ministers' wives. I think my rebellion at being a minister's wife was in reaction to those early experiences, in part.

When my husband and I met in college, my Christian faith was very strong and to be a minister's wife excited me very much. However, looking at that excitement from the manse, I think what I had seen as so exciting was the idea of entertaining people and all the marginal things. At that time, I was very cynical about the church, on top of some personal problems about our marriage, which my lack of participation augmented. So my husband began to feel very alone and unsupported.

Feeling that perhaps the rural dimension of ministry was a major factor of my discontent, I urged my husband to begin to look for a more sophisticated church when he became ready to move. When we did move, I began to participate more for a short period of time, but was basically uninvolved.

During this time, I was working at a demanding job, making what I felt was a career for myself, and I felt good about this.

My husband left this "more sophisticated" church after a short period of time and began to pursue a private practice in a specialty he had developed while I continued to work to support us financially. I had a

definite feeling that being a career woman was what I wanted.

During this time our marital trouble came to a head and my husband was ready to leave me. This crisis was painful and created a time of self-examination. I was involved in individual therapy for a while and as I began to change, my husband and I began marital therapy.

At that time my husband was making some redecisions about his career and accepted a temporary supply pastorate. With many reservations we moved to this church.

As the marital problems began to be resolved, my personal growth has enabled me to really embrace this church community. I am active and involved and feel very rich in being a part of the life of this congregation.

We are in the process of accepting a permanent call here, which is a rural community similar in many ways to our first pastorate, yet very different.

I am very different, too. My faith is again strong. As I become more integrated into the community, I'm discovering that expectations are my projections. The marriage that my husband and I are creating is a strong one and bears a Christian witness.

I have quit my job, as I began to see the emotional price my job demanded. I had to decide on priorities. I knew that my marriage was very important to me, something four years ago I had not yet discovered.

The sexual revolution which has developed in recent decades has permeated the society with both beneficial and harmful attitudes toward sex and sexuality. For the clergy couple, it has meant a greater freedom to accept and express more openly the physical aspects of their marriage. It has

meant, too, less willingness to settle for sexual frustration and greater willingness to seek help in overcoming difficulties. A counselor points out that extramarital affairs among clergy couples appear to be somewhat more common than in previous years. This does not necessarily lead to divorce.

The freedom to be found in society today to develop a life unrelated to marital identification presents opportunities for sexual relationships to both the minister and his wife. At one time the clergy wife was cautioned that her husband would meet alluring and receptive women in the course of his job. Now, the wife can meet other men either at her work or in broad community activities. The traditional teachings of the church for commitment to one's spouse and to the concept of Christian marriage are still valid even though more strongly challenged than before.

There is mutual agreement by both ministers and their wives that the clergy wife has the right to maintain and develop her own unique abilities. The theory sounds easy but the practice is more difficult. Since the clergy wife believes in her husband's vocation, it is harder to protect her rights against its demands. If she yields to the pressure, she may become a "saint," but a frustrated and uninteresting one.

Much depends on the husband and his willingness to be supportive of her. This will involve encouragement and affirmation as well as a reshuffling of time and money. He will be required to practice what he preaches. The greatest single factor for a wife's attempts to reach for further education, to master new skills, and to experience growth is the attitude of cooperation from her husband. She too must pay a price in time and money arrived at on the basis of her own priorities. She must be willing to act in the light of her own lively sense of self-worth. The happiest marriages are those where there is a mutuality of respect.

For the modern clergy wife, there are a multitude of opportunities for personal enrichment. They range from formal and accredited classes on the college or graduate level to all manner of community events. The improvement of the physical appearance in a technical society is available to all. Gone forever can be the dowdy, unattractive clergy wife. Even the least favored can improve upon nature's gifts, often with a smile of approval from the congregation.

MARRIAGE TO A MINISTER—NOT ALL BAD

There are satisfactions to be found by a woman married to a minister. Many of her frustrations are shared with wives of other professional or business men. The uniqueness of her place is emphasized by her participation in her husband's vocation. She can share in his work, his hopes, and dreams so that her involvement becomes an expression of the meaning of life.

Certainly the kind of man who enters the ministry and gives his life to service for others perceives the meaning of commitment. In a relationship that requires personal integrity and responsibility, the clergy wife, for the most part, can rely upon her partner.

Clergy couples have a demanding schedule but theirs is a life filled with opportunity to know persons who enlarge life. Often these persons are leaders in community life or the cultural sphere. Many times they are simply those who have learned to live victoriously over illness, tragedy, or hardship. They stretch the mind and soul of the clergy wife.

Perhaps the greatest satisfaction of all is to be found in identity with and involvement in a task greater than self. Here is a composite of statements made by clergy wives:

"The feeling that in this world we may be doing some good" . . . "The wide scope of life-death-human emotions, tragedies, joys which we face all the time by being intimately involved with other people" . . . "Living a challenging, growing, changing life" . . . "Having opportunities that wouldn't have come about in a less vital profession" . . . "Mainly, that I am part of a team that enriches the lives of people. It also enriches my life to be able to witness for our Lord Jesus Christ."

Many modern couples are writing contracts to make their marriages more equal. Most clergy couples live in covenant that their marriages might be more loving.

Chapter IV

Family Life in a Fishbowl

Just Molly and me
And baby makes three—
or four . . . or more!

Those lines are a parody of songs of decades ago. Now, as then, the majority of marriages lead to the creation of a family unit. The union of a man and a woman ideally is deepened and enriched by the arrival of children. Today, family life is surrounded by perils that threaten to destroy it. In a nationwide survey conducted by a leading magazine, 76 percent of the answers indicated belief that family life in America is in trouble. In spite of the difficulties of family life, 91 percent indicated they would still have children, given another chance.

Once the family was a self-sufficient unit. The children were a part of the labor group which ran the farm and the home for the benefit of the whole. Each person knew that his contribution to the economic well-being was vital. In addition, the family provided love, intimacy, and emotional support. It was broadly based, encompassing several generations, and ties of loyalty and interdependency that included more than the immediate relatives. For the most part, it provided the necessities of life—physical nurture, emotional support, and spiritual development—for its members.

Today, the family is limited in size and scope. Birth control takes care of the first, and the mobility of the population limits most households to parents and their underage children. This new family has been described as a "hedonistic anarchy" where a lack of commitment leads to an attitude that stresses *me* instead of *we*. Members go their own way, and little or no depth communication takes place. Two fundamental pursuits of life—work and raising the next generation—are in conflict for the time and energy of parents. A reliable, constant source of loving support and intimacy is gone—lost in the rush of modern life. For most Americans, however, their children are still their greatest source of satisfaction. Clergy wives have indicated that they are among that number.

People are having fewer children than in the past, but evidence indicates that fewer persons are remaining childless. In fact, childlessness has declined during the past several decades. Clergy families support this with their own statistical evidence. Our results indicate that 92 percent have children. Reflecting the change in modern family size, 74 percent have one to three offspring and only 18 percent have four or more.

PRESSURES INTENSIFIED

With cultural and societal pressures, reaching a critical stage for the survival of the American family, clergy wives have concern for the additional tensions that are a part of life for the clergy family. The difficulty of living a "fishbowl" existence has proved to be a problem in the past, and still is. The advent of a child in the clergy family is a public event which the congregation monitors with interest, ranging from care and concern to curiosity. It does not end with a baby's safe arrival, for "preachers' kids" develop an awareness of being constantly on display. As they grow older, they sense that their conduct often reflects upon their parents' ministry. In many areas the old stereotypes of "P.K.s" have not died and congregational expectations may arouse negative response. One wife says one of her major frustrations deals with

> "The unrealistic expectations of our children to be better than others. We've experienced this already and our children are only two and four."

The clergy wife must often be a buffer between the church community and her children.

It is significant that a committee composed of educators, clergy, and lay persons, while planning a workshop for the observance of the 1979 Year of the Child, indicated that in many ways the clergy family can be categorized as "single parent." The response of clergy wives indicates that they share this view. They said:

> "I especially wish for more help in parenting from my husband, but he's just not physically available."

> "I resent his endless hours. I resent that he never had time to see his children grow up."

> "We have no weekends to enjoy as a family when the children are free from school. He is too busy Saturday

getting ready for church and too busy Sunday with
services to enjoy outings as a family."

The resulting senses of fear, resentment, and sorrow, coupled
with little or no time for pleasure together as a family, develop into tremendous stress for the clergy wife. When she
is employed outside the home the situation is further aggravated.

The clergy father has expectations in regard to his children which are similar to those imposed upon his wife.
He looks to them for a high degree of loyalty and relies
upon them for a significant measure of programmatic support. In their early years this involves their participation
in church school and club activities. In adolescence they
are often the mainstay of youth groups and projects. Depending upon the type of congregational life, these requirements can be either helpful for the child's Christian
growth or an out-and-out detriment. This was the perception of one mother who observed:

"I would like to be raising my children in a larger
church such as the one in which I grew up. For example, one of our children is quite rejecting of the church,
and I sense that one factor is the fact that he is the only
one of his age and sex in the whole congregation."

According to another, this close association to church life
can be injurious:

"Our home centers around the church—what is or is
not happening. Church frustrations become home frustrations and affect tension of family."

FINANCES GO PUBLIC

A television program that explored American family life in 1979 reported that money, or the lack of it, affected the stability and happiness of the home. Money has assumed much symbolic importance in our society. It rarely represents only what it can buy. It can symbolize everything from power and security to prestige and love. Like all symbols, money is misunderstood as it becomes directly related to feelings. Money and feelings are very much tied together.

The salary scale for clergy has been, for the most part, better in recent years, but it is still at the lower end of the societal value system in terms of money. That value system is not based upon the relative importance of the job performed but is determined by the money received. As average persons relate to this value system they tend to measure their own worth by the remuneration received for daily work. The effect upon the clergy has been to lower the value of the job performed with a subsequent lowering of respect for the performer. The family thus becomes the major source of reassurance for his self-esteem, which affects the internal life of the family and their perceptions of one another.

In listing her major frustrations a fifty-one-year-old clergy wife who is employed full time said:

> "My husband does not vent any anger or disappointment on church members but comes home and our oldest daughter and myself receive the full blow."

She lists as her next concern:

> "Trying to live on the money paid."

When the clergy wives list money as one of their major frustrations, they refer to more than just its scarcity.

Certainly the lack of privacy in regard to the finances of the clergy family does not add a helpful dimension to their pursuit of esteem. The whole congregation and colleagues in ministry are aware of their financial position in regard to salary and any fringe benefits they receive. A thirty-four-year-old wife noted that she has:

> "A feeling that our business and life-style is the entire church's business."

And another said there are:

> "Too many bosses [the congregation], pettiness, and resentment by some members toward salary increases and manse improvements."

No doubt the development of duplicating equipment and its widespread use has meant that budgetary details are more broadly distributed and have further eroded the clergy family's privacy.

HOUSING AS SYMBOL

The physical care of the minister and his family by a congregation in terms of salary and housing takes on deep meaning. They symbolize a relationship. In the eyes of the clergy wife, the provision of adequate housing is a measure of congregational regard for her. I remember my own feelings as a young woman living in a variety of church-provided housing. It always seemed that other couples were the recipients of new interior decorating, major improvements, or even new construction, while I never even got to pick a color scheme. Usually, the house had been newly painted or papered just prior to the departure of our predecessor. Deep inside I used to wonder what was wrong with me. "Why doesn't the congregation appreciate me as much as so-and-so's does?" One of my fantasies, only half in jest, was that when I died I would hear the words:

> "Well done, good and faithful servant, enter into the joy of thy $5,000 kitchen."

(Today I would have to dream of three times that amount!)

The methods used by congregations to determine when—and especially what—maintenance will be done to housing assume meaning too. Many times the clergy wife is not consulted beforehand and though she is closest to the scene, her priorities are not considered. Other times she may be asked to submit lists of improvements she thinks important. She may conscientiously compile her suggestions only to find them ignored. By whatever method decisions are reached, if she is not truly a part of the system, the clergy wife views manse care as demeaning, as a means of "put-down," and as an implication of her unimportance, her ignorance, or her greed.

With real estate representing a valid safeguard against the forces of inflation, congregations are exhibiting more interest in caring for clergy housing. The majority of clergy families still live in church-provided housing in spite of a growing trend toward housing allowances. By thoughtful, conscientious upkeep and repair, congregations can do much to enrich the relationship with the clergy family, especially the wife.

IMAGES AND RELATIONSHIPS

Most clergy wives have a deep sense of loneliness and isolation. They feel set apart from others because of their status. They are assigned a symbolic role as the personification of the community conscience. One wife said:

> "People, I think, shy away from me, for example, if they've missed church. It's not much fun to be a walking judgment on others."

This is a type of rejection against which it is difficult for her to react. It may be another reason clergy wives resent their introduction as "our minister's wife" rather than by their own names. It can become a signal to the third party for their response.

Most have experienced in community life this feeling of a curtain falling when their marriage relationship is revealed. One clergy husband in speaking of what he saw as his wife's greatest need replied:

> "She needs a woman friend other than a church member. I am her only close friend. Before I entered the ministry it was easy for her to make female friends, but now she is in a role *created* by others and women tend to shy away from inviting her to social functions or treating her in a normal way. She is a 'minister's wife,' and as such, 'the girls' seem to find it uncomfortable to have her around. She has not changed, but people treat her differently than before I was a minister."

Others in the group tend to monitor their responses so that they become what they perceive to be more acceptable. One wife noted that some people

> "Cannot say certain things or do things in front of me."

There is created, therefore, an unreal relationship. Instead of persons relating to a person, there is the self-imposed response to a perceived role that limits any kind of meaningful or satisfactory association.

The children in clergy families are aware of this feeling of isolation, since they often experience it too. One mother spoke about:

> "Our children's feelings that they're considered different."

I remember in our own family life when our school-age children were reprimanded for some misdemeanor by the teacher, who added:

> "I didn't expect that from you—after all, your father is a minister."

One clergy wife, when asked how the children in a clergy family should be raised to be strong although branded "preachers' kids," said:

> "My own children are bussed to school where few people know their father's occupation, but even so they are constantly challenged to break the rules or be branded goody-goody."

No doubt, for the most part, this discrimination is caused by a conflict of value systems. This tends to become more intense during the teen years when children will attempt to hide their father's occupation because of an awareness of societal views.

There is no question that today's clergy mother must exercise a greater degree of understanding and patience with children who are raised in a highly permissive and affluent culture. She must be more careful than her counterpart of the past not to impose standards and decisions upon her offspring which were arrived at in her maturity. It means that she must often stand as a defense against criticism and exercise ingenuity and even courage to aid in their social development. Some twenty years ago when planning an After the Junior Prom party for our daughters I encountered opposition by some members of the congregation. They voiced objection to this use of church property. I maintained that the manse was our home and, supported by some others in the church, went ahead with the event. It proved to be one of the girls' happier memories.

WHAT SOCIAL LIFE?

There are other impediments to building a social life. One of these is financial. During the early child-rearing years is the time of lowest family income, and so the money to provide baby-sitting is carefully budgeted. Usually, for the clergy family, the sum available is allocated for those times when husband and wife both must attend a church function. (It has been pointed out that clergy couples often spend more time together than most. That time, however, is not spent in what could be termed "pursuits of choice.") The money available for entertaining in a time of rising prices is a factor in the

attempt to provide the climate for developing friendship.
Two observations by clergy wives are worth noting. The first
said that there was

> "Too little money for the social standards of the con-
> gregation and community."

And the other has tried to cope with the problem in this way:

> "Well, while I have small children, while I am involved
> with so many church and nonchurch activities, and
> while we are remodeling the house, I don't really feel that
> gracious little dinner parties are the sort of thing I can
> do—so I haven't. We invite friends (some from church
> and some not) over for hot dogs, Jell-O salad, and cake.
> And that feels good. (Besides, hot dogs fit our budget
> better than 'gracious little dinner parties.')"

Though most clergymen would deny it, there is a sense of
competition among them. Especially in smaller towns where
they all vie for the new families that move in. Then, too, they
do not wish to discuss any problems or admit to any conflict
within the congregation they serve lest they appear unsuc-
cessful in their professional life. The marks of such success
tend to be status symbols, such as million-dollar sanctuaries;
comfortable, modern housing; multiple staffs; higher than
average salaries; membership size; and large attendance at a
variety of services and programs. (The development of such
success measurements cannot be laid exclusively at the door
of the clergy. The laity, and the society at large, also use these
tangible criteria to gauge a minister's worth.)

These tend to be the conversational ingredients when clergymen gather for social affairs. It is depressing for clergy
couples who may have nothing of this nature to share. A wife,

aged thirty-six, with three children, in an urban church, asks these questions:

> "Why is it that neighboring churches seem to feel such a need for competition? Why can't they share programs, outreach, and friendship? We have had as guests in our home at various times several clergy couples new to the area, only to be later informed that we were 'playing into the hands of the opposition.' In nearby suburbs are several families with children the same age as ours. They have large yards, while we have none. How I wish we could be invited for a picnic. . . . Do they feel guilty that some of our former members have joined their congregations? Or do they feel that something our children have experienced in the ghetto schools will rub off?"

Sometimes the clergy husband is not willing to actively build social relationships. In his professional life he is dealing with people all the time. When he has some leisure time he does not desire to be with other persons, feeling that to do so would be an extension of daily routine. This attitude caused one wife to inquire: "But where does that leave me?" Neither can she find satisfaction for her social needs at the church because, as another wife observed, there is

> "The lack of time available for family such as at church family socials when other husbands are helping care for their children, but my husband is expected to be visiting with others or leading the activities."

The time schedule for the clergy family poses another problem. Weekends are the periods of relative freedom and relaxation for most families but are often the busiest for the minister. Evening meetings further erode available time that could be spent with friends. Holidays are a time when special services and events are planned. Trying to observe them with relatives is most difficult if travel is involved. This fact adds to the burden of maintaining contact, let alone relationship, with extended family.

One development of modern life is the longer life expectancy provided by better scientific and medical knowledge. This fact has introduced a new dimension into family care, resulting in considerations involving parents and even one's own plans as one ages. In common with most Americans, clergy couples are usually some geographic distance from their families and homes of origin. An additional burden is created when oversight of infirm parents is needed. Additionally, the assumption of financial obligations for such care places an impossible burden on an already deficit budget. An excerpt from a questionnaire emphasizes this. The writer is sixty-five years old and says:

> "My mother is eighty-seven years old. She lives alone and shouldn't. Meeting her needs is frustrating, as we are not always sure we are doing what is best for her and for us. Our marriage is good. We want to keep it that way."

This longer life-span increases the number of clergy couples who move from the active parish life to retirement. This calls for a number of decisions not faced by others. There is an unwritten rule that the minister must move from the community he has served. If he has no family home or area to which he can return, there must be a total environmental change. Many with no equity in housing find such a move most difficult to arrange and still manage a degree of independence for themselves. In addition, there are the emotional ties to be severed which have developed over a lifetime of service. One sixty-year-old wife recognized this when she requested:

> "Right now I need prayers for adjustment after my husband retires. It will be a change from being active in a congregation, to move to a new congregation and make new friends and have new activities."

Retirement for the clergy husband involves, in a valid way, a form of retirement for his wife as well—especially if she has participated and has been active in congregational life.

MALE PARENTING

Unquestionably, the diversity of today's mores and social customs allows more freedom to adopt a family life-style of choice. The old rigid forms of marriage and family life are changing, especially among young couples. The current human liberation movement which seeks to free both men and women from societal stereotypes has accelerated that change. This is especially noticeable in the whole area of parenting. It is no longer a purely feminine preserve. Fathers are "getting into the act" too. That act is the nurture and loving supervision of a young life.

There are a variety of motivations for this new role for father. Many fathers have memories of their own fathers who did not share their interests, took no responsibility for their care, and were so involved with jobs that they had no energy left for children. The feminist movement is credited with making it more acceptable for men to move out of old images and share in the birth and rearing of their children. Others cite

the trend toward smaller families and the considered decision, shared by both partners, to have a child. Yet another
factor is the decline of the extended family which once eased
some of the mother's tasks. Now, by necessity, men have to
pitch in, particularly since many more women are working.

Determined to make a significant contribution to raising
their children, a number of today's fathers are making career
sacrifices. One third to one half of the men offered promo-
tions or transfers in 1978 turned them down. A significant
factor was their desire to continue their commitment to their
families. Men with less flexible jobs are often frustrated by
their inability to have more family time.

> One clergy father had a busy schedule, there was no
> doubt. He was working for an advanced degree at Har-
> vard, serving a small but active church as pastor, and
> was the father of three growing children. The time
> frame was so tight that he could barely squeeze in a
> good-night kiss for his wife before his eyes closed in
> utter weariness. There always seemed to be something
> that needed doing—a sick call to make, a study paper
> to prepare, a sermon to write. The family came last.
> The children might cry when he left the house for yet
> another reason, but once the door closed behind him he
> didn't hear them anymore. One spring morning he re-
> turned to the house after an absence of four days. There
> was no one on the ground floor, so he ran up the flight
> of stairs to the second floor. As he reached the upper
> hall, a curly head peeked out of the door to his left.
>   "Hi, Daddy, where are you going now? You're al-
> ways off somewhere!"
>   With a start he realized that his four-day absence
> had not been noticed by his child because he himself
> usually wasn't around. Right then he determined that

his schedule would be altered so that he would be at home for at least an hour of "child-awake" time. He said, "It's sad when your own children don't really know whether you are coming or going!" It took a lot of planning and commitment, but he did it.

The implications of this trend for clergy families are significant. While their work hours are demanding in terms of hours and emotional stamina, the clergy do determine their own schedules for the most part. In ancient Rome family life consisted of the artificial acting out of roles which prevented the members from functioning in a warm and human way. This pattern has prevailed for too long. Clergy fathers can aid in the modern impetus toward a tender and whole humanity by their own example. By the same token, mothers in clergy families must insist upon sharing with their husbands in ministry to their own children—a ministry that includes the joys and satisfactions as well as the burdens.

Actions speak louder than words. An act of commitment dramatizes a message so that it becomes fixed in hearts and minds. Martin Luther, when he married Katherine von Bora, was practicing what he preached. The leap of faith which they took turned out to be a glorious blessing for them—as it has for centuries of other pastors and their wives. He viewed the family as a vehicle for Christian witness and as an example to be followed. The growing emphasis upon the importance of the family in current journals indicates that it is far from dead as a social organism. Though it is changing and developing in new and exciting directions, there is still a need for role models to guide the process. Is it a reasonable expectation that the clergy family can fulfill this need? I believe that it is. It will require a rethinking of values and priorities, a new defining of the meaning and method of ministry, and a creative involvement in new forms of Christian nurture.

Chapter V

Wives Who Work

Women have always worked. Especially has that been true in families with low incomes. When the floods of immigrants came to America at the turn of the century, the whole family worked—and that included the sisters and the mothers. During World War II, Rosie the Riveter became a folk figure and symbolized the women who left their kitchens and vacuum cleaners to join the labor force, thus freeing men for the armed forces. Once peace came, these women were expected to return to the domain of the home. For the most part, they did, but a new sense of independence had been aroused. In recent decades a new phenomenon has developed. Large numbers—and they continue to grow—of middle-class wives and mothers are now employed outside the home. Many influences have contributed to this trend.

One of the first agents for change was the development of technology. Much of the production in the past had been carried on by individual women in the home. It is quite a list of jobs: the spinning industry, encompassing the gathering, dyeing, and spinning of wool, flax, and cotton fibers; the manufacture and design of clothing and household needs through weaving, sewing, knitting, and quilting; the food industry, from cultivation and harvest through preparation to preserving. In addition, the woman supervised a staff, whether in the form of paid household workers or members of the extended family. The industrial revolution changed all that. These tasks were moved from the home to the factory on a mass-production basis. Three of the four manufacturing industries employing the largest numbers of workers are textiles, food and related products, and clothing. As a result, the home contains much less creative and satisfying activity. It is small wonder that modern woman searches for new occupations. In order to be human and feel a part of the world, she must do so.

The second has to do with better health care and a longer life expectancy. The dramatic drop in infant mortality has cut in half the number of years spent in childbearing and infant care. For each child that died at the turn of the century, at least three survive today. Women do not need to bear large numbers of children anymore in order to have a family. Modern families, because of better birth-control methods, include, on the average, only two or three children. Consequently, child care has become a small segment of a woman's total life-span. In addition, the revolution in health care has given women the vitality and energy to utilize these years.

At the other end of the scale, life expectancy has increased by about thirty years in this century—years which can be added to those released by the reduction in child care. A further gain is made possible by medical advances which have all but eliminated childhood diseases, introduced the use of antibiotics, and enforced the control of milk and water supplies. Not only is the wife and mother healthier, so is the entire family. The result has been a reduction of the time needed for nursing the sick. The revolution in medicine has made available to modern women the equivalent of virtually a second adult lifetime as compared to the life-spans of their predecessors. A major segment of women's lives, therefore, is no longer filled with activities that characterized adult life in the past.

Another factor is economics. Many employed women are principal wage earners or family heads and work because it is necessary for family support. New patterns of consumption have raised the level of desire for goods, so that more than one earner is required. Additionally, the rising rate of inflation has so increased the cost of all goods and services that many women enter the labor force just to maintain the family standard of living. Then, too, legislative action has mandated nondiscrimination because of sex, thus increasing the number of women workers and adding to the varieties of jobs now open to them.

Also, women work because they desire to use their skills and abilities. Girls are expected to go through the identical educational system as boys and they are pursuing their studies at increasingly higher levels. With more training for the professions and for business, women are becoming interested in higher and broader vocational goals. For many, the greater gravitational attraction comes from outside the home. There is the conviction that they will not be their fully human selves until they establish relationships with the wider world.

EMPLOYED OUTSIDE THE HOME

Evidence indicates that clergy wives are a part of this trend. They are no longer expected to spend their days solely in activities of church and home. In fact, 51 percent of pastors' wives are employed outside the home—a higher percentage than that of the general population. Very few congregations are opposed to the idea of their minister's wife taking on a full- or part-time job. Since ministers often depend upon their wives to provide support during the seminary years, few of them are in a position to resist their spouse's employment.

As they enter the labor market, the wives of ministers bring impressive credentials with them. Their educational level is very high. An overwhelming 82 percent have received collegiate education and 40 percent of that number have pursued postgraduate levels of education. Another 10 percent have received other forms of technical or vocational training. These figures, no doubt, reflect somewhat the value systems of the homes from which they came. Education has always had a high priority in the Christian community.

Their vocational choices also reflect the Christian sense of service and nurture. The largest vocational categories are teaching (with 43 percent of the total), nursing, and social work. Secretarial employment follows closely. The greatest diversity of job classification is to be found in the fifty-to-fifty-nine-year-old segment. It ranges from telephone operator to artist and is the only group that contains a business owner.

One California clergy wife shared with me her own recent quest for employment:

> "As I filled out the application, the question asking about past experience that would contribute to my qualifications stumped me for a moment. Then I thought, my twenty years as a minister's wife have taught me a great deal, so I put it down. I pointed out that in this capacity I had been required to learn how to work with varieties of persons, to cope with criticism, to master new skills, to be flexible in my response to unexpected situations. When I wrote it

all down I recognized the validity of what I said.

"The upshot of it was that I was offered a responsible position with a banking institution. I was told that my experience as a clergy wife had been a determinative factor in my being selected.

"I found a sense of satisfaction and achievement in that. The years I had spent learning so many hard lessons did count in the marketplace."

The major factor that impels a clergy wife to seek employment is economic. Sixty-six percent of the wives indicate that their income is necessary for family support. In counting pension benefits, 71 percent stated that they receive credits which are important for future retirement. In examining their financial needs, the clergy wives have indicated a general concern for the education of their children and for their own retirement needs. One wife notes about her income:

"It is banked for the children's education. I don't see how we could educate our children without my contribution."

In some cases the definition of "family support" determined the answers given. If interpreted strictly in terms of immediate needs such as food and clothing, the women felt their income was not necessary. But many went on to indicate that their earnings did provide for such family items as orthodontal care and vacation expense as well as music or art lessons for the children. One reported:

"As inflation outstrips salary increases, its [extra income] necessity is becoming imminent."

A thirty-two-year-old wife observes that she is currently attending school in preparation for supplementing the family income which is a future necessity.

Anxiety about income for retirement is frequently voiced. The lack of savings and of equity in a home are overriding concerns. One wife says her income is "being put toward a home." Another, in emphasizing the importance of her own pension benefits, says:

> "My husband's benefits are lower because he was forty when he was ordained."

Another cites an obvious irony:

> "I have pension benefits, but due to clergy mobility they will not accrue to benefit us."

One aspect of this trend toward working outside the home has direct bearing upon the traditional primacy of the clergy "call." The replies of the ministers indicate that 50 percent of them would be influenced on relocation by their wife's employment. One said:

> "My wife's income is necessary for family support; she has assured job security in the school district through tenure, and has significant pension credits. To put it bluntly, I have had opportunity to move but we just could not afford to do so."

If the pastoral relationship is satisfactory for both minister and congregation, this decision can be mutually beneficial; but if there are tensions on either side, the stress can become almost unbearable. Further, the sense of responsibility for her husband's professional unhappiness is an additional burden for the working clergy wife.

NOT FOR MONEY ONLY

In addition to economic contributions, employment by clergy wives offers important psychological and emotional benefits. Employed wives usually include in their lists of major satisfactions their jobs and the opportunities thus provided for broader contacts in community life. They express a sense not only of personal fulfillment but of vocational realization as well. They phrase it in this manner:

"I feel I am making a contribution as a public school teacher."

"The enormous challenge of my professional life."

"I have experienced a change for the better mentally since I've been working."

"My satisfactions have little to do with the church but with my own career and personal life."

"I enjoy my job in a personnel office dealing with many people every day. The income from my job has helped to educate our children and also to buy a home, which we just moved into this spring."

"The chance to work again—elsewhere than in the church—as a teacher."

"When I went to graduate school and when I accepted a faculty position, I felt a renewed sense of personal worth, of capability, and of sheer pleasure. It has helped me 'think through' a great deal. I like having a *worthwhile* assignment and seeing it through capably."

One wife, trained as a nurse but now employed as a crisis counselor for victims of rape, expresses her sense of vocation even more forcefully.

"The fulfillment and reinforcement I receive from working with rape victims and in public education on this issue—*this is my ministry.*"

There is an element of escape from demands for every working woman. "I can't do it—I work, you know," has come to be an often repeated phrase. The women's program in local churches was profoundly affected as were community agencies which depend upon the efforts of countless volunteers. For the clergy wife who took a job, a rescheduling of time meant that she could no longer assume the responsibilities traditionally assigned to her. One wife voiced her feelings this way:

"Working full time makes me less susceptible to 'guilt' for not being a typical wife."

Employment also provided her with an opportunity to move beyond the limits she perceived to be imposed upon her as a clergy wife. For example, in explaining the change experienced in the role of clergy wife.

"My beginning to work part time this last year has lessened my involvement at church, i.e., I'm not doing VCS for the first time in eleven years."

The lay persons expressed the fact that their expectations have been influenced by an employed wife of the minister.

> "If, for example, she is pursuing her own 'career' and can't be active in the church or chooses not to be, that's up to her."

EFFECTS ON THE FAMILY

Undoubtedly, working outside the home has had a profound impact upon the role definition of the clergy wife. If employment is what she really wants, there is no reason why she shouldn't try. It is true for her, as for other women, that working may not turn out to be everything that she hoped. For the clergy family, the career stresses can exacerbate an already difficult life.

Often family time, the focus of so much frustration, is further limited because of schedule conflicts. Free periods of various family members do not coincide; this leads to a paucity of recreation or pleasure that involves all. Further, there is limited time to perform necessary household tasks and even less time for real communication and relationship with husband and children. Moreover, both husband and wife tend to be tired and preoccupied. In order to work, the clergy wife needs a high level of energy and a significant measure of good health.

The clergy tend to have a degree of egotism—not in a totally negative sense, for the very nature of the ministry demands an amount of self-regard. It seems very difficult for any man to accept the achievements of his wife if they exceed his own. This applies to either finances or more subtle rewards and recognition. For the clergy it would appear even more difficult—an element of jealousy can creep in.

Further conflict can emerge when the husband is indifferent to or even refuses to share his wife's job responsibilities. In conversation one wife recounted her experience.

> "I've always attended events such as dinners or meetings in the church, the community, or the denomination that my husband expected of me. Now that I'm employed with a social agency, there are similar demands made of me, and of my spouse. He refuses to participate and I have to go alone and make excuses for him. His attitude is stubborn and does not allow for any discussion. It has become a real focus for resentment on my part and is proving destructive of our relationship."

HOUSEWORK PARTNERS

The nitty-gritty details of domestic life provide another area where difficulty arises. Someone has to do the housework—cooking the meals, scrubbing the floors, doing the laundry. Two aspects of anger surface in this regard. One is the male resistance to change in the perceived gender definition demanded by the assumption of "female" tasks. The other is the woman's moving away from these duties with a sense of release from second-class status. As a result, feelings will often run high over trivial issues.

For the dual-career clergy family, congregational attitudes can range from hostile to supportive. The implication may well be drawn that the minister is neglecting his significant calling to pursue unimportant work. Other men in the congregation may feel that their own gender identity has been threatened by the role model projected by the pastor. For young men today, the concept of husband is largely based upon the ideas of their fathers, who got the ideas from their fathers. So these images are at least three generations old. It is not easy to adjust to new forms and patterns. Even here the minister can willingly serve as a positive role model.

How can the couple deal with the issue of housework? The first suggestion is to list all the household chores. Usually this helps to clarify the understanding of what needs to be done. Second, the couple should make independent and joint judgments about availability for a task, plus the interest and skill needed to perform it. Third, there should be an equitable division of labor. There will be some tasks neither husband nor wife will want to do. These they can either divide equally or hire someone else to perform. Once these practical problems are resolved, the crisis atmosphere should dissipate, allowing the partners to meet and relate on an equal footing.

Financial and economic benefits can also become a stumbling block unless there is a clear understanding about joint funds. Conflict emerges if discussion descends to the level of "his" and "her" incomes. This was apparent when one young wife said:

> "I'm going to get a professional window washer. Our windows are so dirty and it will only cost forty dollars."

Her husband objected on the grounds that it was an unnecessary expenditure for a job they could do themselves. With her eyes flashing, she replied:

> "Well, it's my money and I'll do it if I want to!"

Communication and agreement over financial priorities and goals are of supreme importance. There is a need to guard against setting priorities on the basis of salary considerations alone. One wife indicated:

> "Now I feel we live in tandem, in support of each other, although his career choices take precedence over mine, since I cannot earn as much as he does."

This raises the question: What if the reverse is true? Should money decide? The clergy wife who thinks all her problems —or even a few of them—are going to be solved by working outside her home for a part of each day is bound to be disappointed.

WORKING AS A VOLUNTEER

Work has been defined as activity in which one exerts strength or faculties to do or perform something. In that light, work cannot be limited to those who receive remuneration for their labors. The secret lies not in doing what everyone else is doing but in doing what is uniquely right for oneself. Therefore, the 49 percent of clergy wives who are not employed are also involved in work.

The whole area of volunteer activity was listed by clergy wives. There was a noticeable difference in types of involvement between the employed and the nonemployed. They could be charted in this manner:

Nonemployed	*Employed*
1. Mostly in area of caring ministries, i.e., Meals on	1. Church Activities
	2. Of a limited nature, i.e.,

Wheels, Hospital
Auxiliary, Tutoring,
Homes for the Aging, etc.
2. Related to their children,
i.e., Scouting, PTA,
School Concerns, etc.
3. Community Groups, i.e.,
Library Friends,
Community Concerts,
Cancer Society, etc.
NOTE: Church activities were
generally not considered
as in same category

Fund Raising,
Special Programs
3. Related to Job Interests,
i.e., Social Workers—
Children's Agencies;
Musicians— Choir
Directors; Physicians,
Medical Society;
Hairdresser—Cuts
Hair for Shut-ins
4. Related to their children,
i.e., PTA, Scouts

There is an apparent consensus that wives need to be as selective about volunteer work as about a paying job. They are, after all, giving of time and of themselves. They therefore sense a right to choose that which interests them and makes them happy. This includes their involvement in the church and its activities. One young wife with a master's degree in religious education said:

> "I have always done my own thing as a clergy wife. I think it is important that your husband support you in the things you want to participate in, but not have hurt feelings if you choose not."

TOWARD SECURITY

Changes in the financial aspects of the ministry bear upon today's clergy wife. Recent gains can alleviate some of the resentment felt by wives. The enactment by denominational judicatories of minimum salary standards for the clergy has brought some measure of parity. The man who serves a small congregation is thus protected from exploitation, and his family with him. The inclusion of study leave is a relatively new innovation that provides the clergy an opportunity for personal growth and enrichment. Most of the seminaries that provide continuing education invite, even encourage, spouse participation. There is no question that this recognition of need for mutual growth is of benefit to today's clergy wife. Its meaning could be further enhanced by financial provision for her tuition and board.

The trend toward a housing allowance with which the pastor may buy his own house can be a mixed blessing. In many communities adequate housing is either unavailable or far beyond the resources of most ministers. Some denominations are establishing funds to assist with the high down payments demanded by lending institutions. For the clergy couple willing to invest themselves in what has been termed "sweat equity" there is an alternate solution. This means that they provide physical labor for the building of a new home or the remodeling of an old one. This can take many forms, depending upon the skill levels of the persons involved. It can mean something as simple as putting insulation in place to more complicated carpentry such as building cabinets. At current pay scales this can be a sizable dividend. There are tremendous satisfactions to be realized from having physical evidence of effort spent for those involved in a profession that has so many intangible rewards. Embarking upon such a project or the maintenance chores of home ownership may stretch an already tight time schedule to the breaking point.

The retirement years are regarded as a tenuous financial period filled for some with dread. Though Social Security coverage has been extended to the clergy and increased pension benefits are being paid, the benefits do not keep pace with current inflationary costs in many cases. A wife aged fifty-six, and, significantly, a recent college graduate, looks to that period with a strong sense of apprehension:

> "I can no longer volunteer services—I have a need to be paid for my work—have been advised that our retirement years will be grim financially if I can't supplement the present state of affairs."

No other group has had so violent a change and challenge as the women of our century. In our day we are confronted, as never before, with the opportunity to choose a style of life in which relationships are given more of a chance. Interestingly, this area has long been regarded as the prerogative of women. There are two principles involved—the principle of equality which asks for the right to be different without being regarded as inferior, and the principle of individuality which asks for the opportunity to develop the enormous range of human potential.

The clergy wife, in most major ways, is engaged in the struggle. She strives to be considered as an individual human being whose aspirations are not limited by sex or marital relationship but by capacity. She seeks rewards that are spiritual as well as monetary. This is another way of saying that she lives in covenant with God and with her fellows. The clergy wife "worker" at home or in the world affirms this belief by her own way of life.

Chapter VI

Does Anybody Care?

The phone rings just as the day begins. Somewhere death has reached out for a member and the pastor is needed ... Filled with breathless excitement, a young couple make an appointment for premarital counseling... A husband and wife troubled in their marriage visit the pastor's study ... A member facing major surgery grips the pastor's hand as they pray together.

These are all scenes from the life of a minister. The image of the church, Biblically and in the world, is of a flock cared for by a shepherd. Christ's last words to his disciples commanded them to feed his sheep. As the church grew and became organized, the assignment of the "shepherd," or pastoral function, was given to the clergy.

Through the centuries this task has assumed many forms and in today's world is more complicated. Generally, however, the role of the pastor can be outlined in this way. He is given the responsibility to:

Confront persons with their spiritual needs and responsibilities;

Assist persons to grow in their faith;

Minister to persons in times of need, such as marriage, sickness, death, conflict, relocation, etc.;

and thus to

> Exemplify the church fellowship and ministry;
> Be a source of guidance and information;
> Fulfill ceremonial tasks.

That the church has survived for centuries affirms the wisdom and the faithfulness of generations of the clergy.

Martin Luther first emphasized the role of all Christians, laity as well as clergy, to be priests and pastors to their fellow believers. In varying degrees, local congregations relate to one another in this very personal and spiritual way. Often this is evidenced most clearly in times of tragedy or crisis rather than on the basis of the joys and sorrows of daily life.

WHEN THE PASTOR'S FAMILY NEEDS A PASTOR

One of the most poignant questions to be answered by the clergy wife is this one: "Upon whom would you call for pastoral care?" It is interesting to note that on questionnaire replies the clergy wives interpreted the term "pastoral care" as being involved with the whole area of problem resolution. Only a very small number mentioned other aspects. In their responses to other questions, however, the whole area of pastoral care was described, often by its lack.

A significant number indicated that either they did not know or there was no one to whom they could turn. Another pastor was named as a likely resource but this was viewed, even by those giving this answer, as less than ideal. One shared this:

"I can get pastoral care from another pastor by calling and making an appointment. But by the time I get there, the pastor is so worried that my marriage is falling apart or my children are dying or something really terrible is going on that he is relieved to hear my 'little problem.' Then the problem is not dealt with seriously. This has happened in several situations with different pastors, so I don't think it was just a fluke. Ordinarily people can get pastoral care on a much lower key, a much more casual level than a pastor's wife can."

The majority indicated that they would turn to their husbands. In commenting upon this response, a seminary professor of pastoral counseling said:

"I suspect that most wives felt this was the expected answer or they might appear disloyal to their husbands. I question the clergy ability to deal effectively with any serious problems in their own family life. After all, there is the wearing of two hats—spouse or parent and pastor. There is valid reason for questioning the objectivity of a professional person dealing with loved ones. That is no doubt why doctors and lawyers have bans against doing so.

"Unfortunately, the pastor will often assume a level of competency that is unrealistic. Out of loyalty, the spouse will adopt the same attitude."

The problem of confidentiality is a very real one and reflects the dread felt about disclosure of conflict in the minister's life. The perception of themselves as expected to "have it all together" inhibits efforts to seek help. Caught in this dilemma of where or to whom to turn, one wife had this experience:

> "I don't really know whom to call upon and that is a big problem to me. Over a year ago I sought support from a session member, which was all right as far as it went, and that person was able to keep her mouth shut. I feel now that this was a rather dangerous thing to do."

Going to a third party in the person of a judicatory executive is viewed as a dangerous risk. Though many would be qualified to help, they are often looked upon as more "political" than "pastoral." The fear that revelation of difficulty would alter the opinion of one who is related in terms of the husband's professional life and career is universally present. Any concept of an executive as a "pastor to pastors" is highly unrealistic.

At a time when marital conflict among clergy couples and the frequency of divorce are increasing, the wives indicate more willingness than in the past to seek help from agencies other than the church. There is the indication of recourse to therapists, psychiatrists, and psychologists for varieties of serious family problems. No doubt these provide healing in extreme cases. In terms of the need to be listened to and advised on the basis of intimate friendship, the clergy wife is very much alone.

ISOLATED IN JOY AND GRIEF

Life is not made up of problems only but of a series of events marked by pain and gladness that are the foundation for growth and maturity. For such happenings, the clergy wife and her family are in a peculiar position as they cope.

The very lack of what has been termed "friends" by the great majority of clergy wives makes celebration or grieving a difficult and very private occurrence. A few anecdotes from clergy families may illustrate this reality.

I

She had found the lump a week before. It was low, on the right side of her breast. A visit to the doctor had confirmed its presence. Without hesitation, the doctor, a member of the congregation, made the arrangements for her to enter the hospital. Today she had been X-rayed as an outpatient so that the surgeon would have as much information as possible. The specialist in the radiology department had questioned her gruffly. Then he had said, "I don't see how anything so extensive could just show up!" With that he had dismissed her.

His words had frightened her. When her minister-husband picked her up outside the hospital, she fought to keep her self-control. She knew he was frightened, too. That night when the house was dark, she stretched on the bed in the spare bedroom and sobbed. She felt utterly alone. There was no pastor, except her own husband, to whom she could talk about her fears and no close woman friend to share her feelings of rage, dread, and helplessness.

II

She was a beautiful girl—at least her parents thought so. She had coped with the demands of life in a minister's family through her teen years to emerge as a caring, open adult who had suddenly fallen in love. She was making her wedding plans. "Daddy," she said. "You've been my minister all my life but this time I want you to be my father. I want you to come down the aisle with me and give me away. We'll just have to get someone else to perform the ceremony."

When the guest list for the reception was being prepared another question arose. "Do we have to invite the whole congregation?" she asked. "I don't want my wedding party to be just another church social. After all, it is my wedding." The compromise was made that the church officers would receive invitations and they would represent the congregation. It was later that the clergy wife heard the gossip.

"They certainly were exclusive, weren't they? I wonder how you rated an invitation?"

"Must have wanted a lot of gifts to have invited so many!"

The climax was reached several days after the wedding when both parents were emotionally exhausted. In the morning mail the letter had arrived. It was anonymous and a bitter attack about the way the whole affair was handled.

Tearing the letter to shreds was not adequate release for the new emotions that surfaced—anger and deep disappointment. And there was no one to talk to about them!

III

Mother had been ill in the manse on Main Street for a long time. Since her daughter was an only child, the burden for her care had been the clergy wife's alone. Finally, one night, death had come. The funeral was a simple affair. The clergyman was from a nearby congregation. He didn't know Mother and was barely acquainted with her daughter. Only a handful of church members came. Later, no one came to listen compassionately to the grief over the loss experienced by the last person to have known the clergy wife as a child.

IV

It was their wedding anniversary, the silver one at that! Surely the occasion should be marked by some celebration. But whom to invite?

V

She wanted to do something to show her caring concern. John and Mary were friends—more than most —and had shared dinner and a few outings. They had grown up in the town and had friends that went back to youthful days. There just wasn't room now for the clergy wife. The intimate circle had closed. She sensed that her friendship was not needed. The relationship with her was an "extra," not a "treasured" one.

VI

They were going to retire in a month. Their plans were to move into an apartment three hundred miles away. "I have mixed feelings," she said. "I hope my health allows me to find a place in a new church home. It sounds silly, I know, but I should hate to be buried by strangers."

Pastoral care should be the hallmark of the Christian church—that institution which is not the message of the gospel but its vehicle. A relationship to that body is an important ingredient for the life of the believer in Christ. Worship and learning are a part of the fellowship. The clergy wife needs this education and discipline as fully as anyone else and yet her affiliation is vastly different from the experience of others. Her own sense of commitment, however, requires a free and participating membership.

In the first place, during her adult years she normally has no change of pastor. It is an unusual circumstance if an individual lay person does not experience the arrival of a new preacher to the church with its resultant challenge and opportunity for growth. This is occasioned by a new face, a new personality, new insights, a new preaching style, new experiences, new leadership. The clergy wife, on the other hand, moves with the minister. Hers is the experience of the same pastor in a new setting.

She has little or no choice about her church membership. Her husband's professional decision usually and automatically decides her relationship. One wife said:

"I have no real church that I can choose on my own apart from my husband's job. I have no pastor apart from my husband."

It is a classic irony of the life of the clergy wife that the people who strive in every way to attract and please members in the church take her for granted. Another wife expresses it this way:

> "The shock of moving—having recently moved from a vital and warm congregation to one that needs to grow and move but just needs to be stirred up—leaves a void in me. It will be filled again eventually, but if I weren't a minister's wife, I wouldn't have had to give up the church of my preference."

The clergy wife has little feeling that her membership is a prize to be sought. During the years of my husband's ministry, I have never been asked by a lay person or an officer to affiliate with the congregation. I have a feeling that I was part of the moving, like all the boxes of books deposited in the study.

NEED TO BE APPRECIATED

One of the joys of life is being appreciated. This seems especially important to participants in congregational activity. Often it falls to the pastor to express this gratitude publicly. Usually, for a variety of reasons, this does not include his wife. A clergy wife who has been involved in serving expressed herself in this manner:

> "I need to have the recognition for doing a job well —not in words always but in a sense of appreciation that I receive. I need to feel people *care* about me and my problems; I need to feel that my ideas are worth *considering* at least; I need to feel that *others* feel I am dependable, reliable, and a good friend be-

cause of who *I* am and not because I'm the minister's wife. Congregations need to know that the
clergy wife is *just like everybody else*—she has needs
and doubts sometimes; she gets tired of going to
meetings and smiling; she needs close friends (in and
out of the congregation); she deserves compliments
for a job well done."

A fraction of the wives have chosen a different course—
one that may be a portent of the future. One wife, in fact,
asked if the solution might be the following:

"I feel a great need for spiritual growth of my own.
Even though I have defined myself as 'just another
member of the congregation,' I find it very hard to act
that way. Ideally, I think a pastor's wife should be a
member of a different congregation from the one to
which her husband is pastor."

The spouse of a pastor in an area ministry involving six
churches states:

"I have joined another church [of the same denomina-
tion] nearby. This is a recent decision and I am pleased
with it."

Her experience is shared by the wives of church bureau-
crats who are free to unite with a congregation of choice.
Another who defines herself as an "atypical clergy wife"
simply says:

"In this parish, I have chosen not to join the local
congregation because of its lack of a sense of mission.
There are some who criticize me for not joining the

church, but there are others who respect my right to express my concern in this way."

The whole aspect of differences is most difficult for the clergy wife to handle. If lay persons find themselves in serious opposition to theological or procedural matters with the pastor or the congregation, they can ultimately withdraw and join another church. The wife of a minister has no such easy solution—she is stuck in the situation and must either resolve it or live with it. These questions usually revolve around theology, methods, and life-style.

The theological concepts, in the past, have been the realm of the pastor. His wife was expected to accept his instruction and insight. (A few of the lay responses reflect this perception.) With a rise in her educational level, the wife has been taught to think for herself. Like many in the congregation, she no longer accepts her husband's analysis without question. This may be why one wife listed as her major frustration:

"Differences in beliefs with church and husband."

The average wife is not involved in her husband's job. She does not have any knowledge of his performance, nor does she offer any critique of it. For the minister, however, his wife is deeply involved in his work and yet can seldom directly influence his professional success. This aspect has no doubt caused one wife to say:

"I need to know what to do when I disagree with the way my husband handles situations, or be able to make suggestions on how to accomplish more and better things in the church without making him feel like I don't believe in him."

FACING UP TO TABOOS

When one becomes a minister, there may be a certain adoption of taboos about conduct or these may be thrust upon him by the congregation. The spouse may not share this feeling or accede to these prohibitions. Thus conflict about forms of recreation or other matters may arise. The younger clergy wives are more openly questioning of the double standard imposed upon them by circumstances.

Joys and sorrows are like the emotional barometers which measure life. Clergy wives experience them profoundly, as we can see from this expression of life by one of them.

> "In one of the Avery and Marsh introits is the line: 'Hey, hey, anybody listening? . . . Anybody care?' I guess my deepest need is to know that, somehow, all the hassle and heartache we go through month after month is worth it. Sometimes I wonder if we are really able to communicate God's love to some of the people with whom we deal. Have I really made a difference in anybody's life? Why can't the session sense what it is the church should really be about? My husband comes home discouraged because of the constant complaints of 'Membership isn't growing' or 'Receipts are off.' The church's neighborhood isn't changing, it has changed! The people are not employed; welfare provides little on which to tithe!
>
> "Almost nobody seems to feel that a minister or his wife needs the same sort of emotional support that other people need. For example, last year's vacation Bible school wasn't perfect, but it opened its doors to more children than had attended in either of the two previous years. Because my co-director's husband needed unexpected surgery at the last minute, I had to

do much more than I had counted on doing. I finally telephoned every name on the church list in search of enough teachers and helpers. At the end of the two weeks, nobody—not one person—said something like, 'You really worked hard on this,' or 'Isn't it nice that so many children who don't attend any church came to Bible school?' All I heard were complaints about every aspect of the program. I cried and cried.

"I find I am crying as I type this. I guess the hurts and criticisms of the past three years are still pretty real. Yet both my husband and I know that we aren't 'done' here and we don't sense that we will be called upon to move for a couple more years, and I know that I have grown because of what I have been called upon to face."

From the depths of suffering to the heights of gladness, life is an emotional pilgrimage. I would be less than truthful if I did not point out that there ought to be expression of gratitude by clergy wives for the kindness and love, the concern and help they received when least expected. One wife says it in her own way.

"Urge the younger wives not to look upon the congregation as THE ENEMY, but as their friends; the congregation will generally respond in kind. I have many fond memories of countless acts of kindness by church members when our children were young and I really needed the help and the friendship given. They always came through just when I needed them the most. God bless them all!"

Chapter VII

No Longer
a Wife

Marriage has held a place of utmost importance in the Christian church. Marked by ceremony and celebration, it is perhaps the most public of religious rites. Early in its history the church developed a paradoxical view of marriage. On the one hand, the monastic orders, with their church-imposed vows of chastity and celibacy, held a higher religious status than the married laity. On the other hand, marriage was regarded as a Christian sacrament employed by God as a means of grace.

Martin Luther in the early days of the Reformation challenged both theses as incompatible with sound theology and Biblical teaching. Luther placed emphasis upon his view that marriage is grounded in the realm of creation and not redemption. In his opinion, marriage is a wonderful blessing of God but it is not a Christian sacrament. This position assigned jurisdiction over marital matters to civil rather than to ecclesiastical authorities. Public officials were to be constantly aware that marriage legislation is a trust from God. In addition, Luther viewed the union of husband and wife as an estate of faith in which the Christian vocation can be practiced.

This concept of marriage continued through the centuries.

The recognized agent for dissolving the marital bond was death. From the beginning, there were two aspects of the death concept when applied to marriage: the first was the death of the marriage relationship itself, resulting in divorce; the second was the death of the marriage partner, resulting in widowhood.

THE DEATH OF THE MARRIAGE RELATIONSHIP

In dealing with the first aspect of the end of a marriage, the church has been involved in controversy as it sought to understand and interpret the teaching of Christ. One approach was to adopt a rigid attitude which denied all consideration of divorce except for adultery or desertion. In that case a further condition was added: only the innocent party might remarry. For generations this was the stance, not only of the church but of society as well. The problem of determining guilt and innocence proved formidable. Caught in the tension between idealism and realism, scholars and theologians sought an ethical decision.

Human perceptions of the human condition have expanded as we pursued the sciences, both natural and social. Our deeper understanding of ourselves and our needs have led to a new evaluation of the marriage relationship. Some modern theologians point to Jesus' emphasis upon man before laws or customs—as recorded in the second chapter of Mark—as a decisive factor. They also emphasize repentance, forgiveness, and love as essential ingredients for the Christian life whether one is married, single, widowed, or divorced.

Christians were faced with two extremes in society. One closed the door to all compromise and encased the matter in a narrowly defined legalism. The other was a totally permissive posture that set no limits and opened the way to what amounted to consecutive polygamy. There is no question that modern society has moved farther toward the latter.

To find a valid basis for Christian action, many individual Christians found that rigid rules are not a satisfactory answer. An aloof, literalistic standard seems to give way when confronted with live human beings and a living Lord. The church, therefore, moved to a more humane and compassionate judgment toward divorce because there were so many variables in marriage situations which made each case unique.

Few contemporary families are untouched by the divorce statistics. Estimates that one in three marriages will end in the courts are not unrealistic. A friend reported that, as a counselor at summer camp, she discovered that fewer than twenty children in a group of eighty were living with both of their natural parents.

THE CLERGY FAMILY AND DIVORCE

The relaxation of societal pressure regarding the death of the marriage relationship has touched the clergy couple as well. Not too long ago, any minister who had been divorced found it difficult to secure a pastorate. This is not true today. In fact, ecclesiastical oversight of clergy marriage by judicatories no longer pertains. As a result, there is no data on the actual number of divorced clergy couples. The responses from a variety of agencies, representing different denominations, indicate that the rate of divorce among the clergy has been increasing at a noticeable pace.

Not all marriages that are in trouble end in divorce. The questionnaire replies indicate that 10 percent of the clergy wives consider their marriage as unstable. One forty-seven-year-old wife, married twenty-five years, indicated "Too many!" as to the number of years spent as a clergy wife. She went on to say:

> "We're still married but are currently in counseling."

One reason unhappy situations continue is economic. A forty-eight-year-old has been a clergy wife for twenty-one years and voiced this statement:

> "I have to bear the brunt of a husband's frustrations and have to cope with a man who is dictatorial, explosive, and jealous. I worry because I am dependent on my husband's health insurance. Wives have worked for years in the church, yet have no rights to adequate medical protection and pension if they want to leave an unbearable situation."

The financial and legal complications arising from pension survivorship benefits for divorcées are not easily solved. There is the view that a divorced spouse is entitled to a survivor's pension based on credits accrued during the period of the marriage. Perhaps the denominational pension agencies will be requested increasingly to examine such proposals in ratio to the growing divorce rate.

There are certain aspects of divorce that affect the clergy couple more than others. Psychologists point out that there is a classic sequence of reaction to the death of a marriage—relief, guilt, and regret. Clergy are often called upon to help persons in their congregation cope with these emotions as they separate. Since there is no pastor for the clergy couple, they must often deal with their feelings in a "do-it-yourself" mode.

The Italians have a phrase, *la bella figura,* which means in essence "putting the best face forward." Clergy and their spouses have become masters in the art. They hide all manner of conflict and trauma with an air of self-control and optimism. This incorporates a high degree of conflict and failure denial which seems a part of clergy self-perception. It is not until the marriage relationship has reached a moribund state that the process of dealing with reality occurs.

The touchy task of getting unmarried is generally more difficult for clergy couples. Redefining relationships with family and friends is complicated by the addition of the congregation. In that sense, the minister's whole professional contact must be realigned and renegotiated.

A CASE STUDY

An examination of a marriage dissolution from the perspective of the wife and the husband might help to interpret the feelings, needs, and perceptions of a clergy couple.

Kate

At the very outset I need to express anger—so much that it wants to pour out. My first anger is directed toward myself and my own lack of maturity. Beyond that is my bitterness at a system that encourages female dependency. I came from an affluent, protected background, so that I was very naive and innocent. I believe I suffered from what I call the "good little girl" syndrome. I wanted to do what was expected of me and please everyone.

Then there is my anger at the church. This rage focuses on a letter that was sent to eight hundred members of the congregation informing them of our marital problems. The decision to do so was made by the session and a church executive who presided at the meeting. I was not present. I should have objected when I first saw it. I had the feeling that this made our family difficulties a "piece of meat" to be chewed over by the whole community. I was overwhelmed with the sense that my privacy had been so brutally violated that I even found myself contemplating suicide. It developed in me a feeling of empathy for the powerless. The hardest thing I ever did was to go to church the Sunday following the mailing. There was a minority of the members who shared my pain, but for the most part people were upset. When someone's marriage fails, other people are forced to face their own. In many ways this is frightening.

Both of my parents were minister's children and they had siblings who went into the ministry. When I married, it wasn't as though I didn't know what that life was like. I was a new college graduate when I married Charles, who had had one year in seminary. To everyone, including our parents, we were the ideal couple. I worked in the seminary library during the next two years, and all seemed well when we moved into our first parish.

I know now that the stereotype of the minister's wife's role is fantasy, but I played the part. As long as I did so, there was peace. As long as I made no demands, I was a dependable source of support.

Then I had some frightening experiences in which I lost touch with reality. I found myself unaware that the children were truly mine. So I went into therapy. My growth from that point was the beginning of the end. I decided to stop my eternal smiling and doing what others wanted. I recognized my need to grow up and become independent of my family. I could not share any of this with Charles. Our marriage was an extreme case of noncommunication.

The children are with me. They are teen-agers who are still active in the church. They have suffered through this "dying" process and, having no pastor, have been ministered to by their friends and members of the congregation. The fact that we have stayed in the community and in the church has been both a help and a hindrance for them. At least they did not have to tear up their roots, and they have been able to maintain a continuing relationship with their father.

I know I am more fortunate than many. The economic options are very grim for most clergy wives who are divorced. Without the financial support of my parents, who could easily afford it, which paid for further education for me, I would have had to take any kind of job to survive.

Psychologically I could not dissolve my marriage until the final divorce decree was granted. Prior to that, I felt the congregation, collectively and in some cases individually, was manipulative toward what they saw as a happier, more moral solution.

My relationship to God has been vital to my adjustment to my new status. I still have relationships in the church which are important to me, although there are those which will never be the same. I honestly think that "no-fault" divorce is really impossible in the psychological sense in the Christian church. I decided to face the issue head on, and that is why I've stayed. If one leaves, it is easier for onlookers to choose up sides.

I felt I had to discover what had happened to me in relation to the congregation. I belong to a small family-like group which has been a source of growth for me. They helped me to realize that anger is really fright, at least in my case. I was desperately afraid of losing my identity.

I have received a master's degree which will help me realize some of the goals I have in view. I would contemplate marriage again but *not* to a minister. In fact, I've told my friends that if they see me look twice at a clergyman, to hit me over the head with a baseball bat!

I am convinced that coping with the trauma of divorce involves the whole concept of self-worth and love. I think this can be directly affected by the cause for the death of the marriage. My present insight is that if you are accustomed to running away, it will take forever to resolve your problems. You will probably run into a shaky second marriage. I feel I now have a greater self-knowledge that opens the possibility to deeper and better relationships. I'm not a "little girl" woman anymore—I'm trying to grow up. I'm going to make it!

Charles

Now that I am in this boat, I find there are many in it with me. Some of the men who have been "heroes" to me because they are great teachers, or preachers, or social activists have also suffered the pain of a divorce. I'm also aware that our number seems to be growing. It seems to me this is a phenomenon, to which the church needs to direct some attention. In addition, I've noted that there are many pastors' sons who are being divorced. It's almost like a fallout or domino effect.

I am a pastor's son and grew up in the manse. I was the second son in our family and I was very anxious to please—both my earthly father and my heavenly one as well. In a real way, my call to ministry is tied to my father. I think I was never quite sure of his love.

I led a very sheltered life and when I married at twenty-two, I was a physical virgin and an attitudinal one as well. For that reason, I think I was locked into a marital commitment by very innocent sexual activity. Petting decided my course because of a sense of both guilt and responsibility.

Because I had decided to become a minister, I looked for a "good minister's wife." Kate really filled the bill. She was very articulate, was active in campus religious life, and came from a family of church leaders. I believe we were married for good reasons, but, as life and people change, so our marriage just dissolved.

Let me say that I support the feminist movement. Women have a just and legitimate claim to struggle against the limitations that have been imposed on them. I say that very honestly. The problem was that I just can't live with a feminist. I guess I felt that it wasn't part of the original contract. I think that Kate was so caught up in feminism that she went through an adolescent phase of throwing off all constraint.

We went through a great many differences of opinion which she aired openly. I couldn't handle that. As I developed a lack of trust in her, my confidence about our marital relationship was eroded and I withdrew into myself. She is a brilliant person. I did not feel her match intellectually in any argument, and that was, in a sense, humiliating. I felt like a nonperson. My reaction was to make her a nonperson too. This was over a two- or three-year period.

I agreed to go into marital counseling and it was a hell for six months. We would engage in verbal clawing at the sessions and continue it when we left. I had lost hope after the first month but continued to go.

One icy cold morning after a session I was sitting at my desk with a member of the church staff. She had said to me: "What gives with you and Kate? People are beginning to talk openly in the congregation."

I was deeply depressed. I thought my pretense had been successful and that our agony was well covered. I felt incapable of action.

A member of the church came to see me at that point. I don't even remember what it was about. She was and is a good friend to both Kate and me, but really closer to Kate. In the course of the conversation she said, "Charles, if you need anything, please feel free to call on me."

Suddenly I began to cry. The tears just flooded out and I sobbed and rocked back and forth because of my inner turmoil. After a few minutes, I felt I was in control again and raised my eyes. She stood up to go and I came around the desk to go to the door with her. All at once I began to sob again, great sobs from deep inside that bent me almost double. She put her arms around me like a mother comforting a hurt child. I cried like that for twenty minutes while she continued to quietly hold me. She was truly Christ to me that day.

After that experience I knew something had to be done. I suggested that Kate go to stay with her parents. She refused. Her parents are very extraordinary people. They told me to come and be with them while we sought a solution. So I moved in with them while Kate and the boys remained in our home.

This was not really satisfactory, as the distance to commute was quite a factor. I got a tiny apartment in the community. There I had a really liberating experience. I am not a mystical person, but while in prayer, I was strongly aware of God's presence. The conviction came to me—"Charles, no matter what, I will not reject you. I love you and you are my child."

From that moment I decided divorce was the only way to go. I had no idea of the church stand regarding divorced ministers, but felt I had no other option. Meanwhile, our living arrangements had been the focus of much conjecture and gossip. Once I had made my decision, I felt the talk needed to be dealt with. Consequently, at a called meeting of the session, we considered alternatives. We felt there were three: (1) Decide it was no one's business but Kate's and mine and make no response to the congregation. (2) Announce the plans for divorce at a church service. (3) Write a letter to the members. The session decided upon the last and appointed a committee to draft it.

It was to contain four elements: Admit the fact that a divorce was imminent; ask the members not to engage in speculation or gossip; if there were questions, talk them over with a member of the session; and pray for God's will. They wanted to indicate prayer for a reconciliation, but I influenced them against that request.

I showed the letter to Kate and she agreed, so it went out. It was like a bombshell. My own feeling was that it was better to have an official word from the ruling body.

The congregation has been extraordinary. One very influential individual was very manipulative. He is well known in the community, is very vocal, and took a rigid position against all divorce. He withdrew from the church but has since rejoined. The whole disruption of pastoral relationship was personally painful to me.

Kate's continuing presence in the congregation is very difficult for me to handle and I feel she makes no attempt to keep a low profile. The boys have suffered through all this, but since they have many other role models—grandparents, aunts, and uncles—they have survived. I try to stay close to them, see them almost every day, and try to be open about my feelings and needs.

It is my belief that clergy and their families need to deal with their pretenses that all is well when, in fact, it is not.

I hope to remarry someday. The divorced clergyman, I am discovering, has a real problem dealing with his sexuality and its expression. I felt release and enjoyed my sense of freedom when the divorce was first final. Now I almost long for intimacy with a woman.

I am sure that for me the sun will shine again.

THE DEATH OF THE MARRIAGE PARTNER

The other aspect, the irrevocable end to the marriage relationship, comes when one of the partners dies. When this happens, the testimony from millions is that the one left behind dies a little, too. There are stages to the grief which are a part of healthy response to loss. It is felt both for the dead and for oneself. Many psychologists point out that one cannot become whole and alive again until the entire sequence of the grief process has been passed through. This takes longer for some than for others. Life-expectancy figures for a husband and wife vary depending upon their respective ages. The actuarial tables used by the Board of Pensions of the United Presbyterian Church indicate that at age 65, a man's life expectancy is 17.9 years. If his wife is age 60, her life expectancy is 25.1 years. Therefore, if they each live for precisely their life expectancy, a rather unlikely assumption, the wife will spend 7.2 years as a widow.

One of the major decisions faced by the clergy widow arises if she and her husband lived in church-provided housing. She must move, there is no choice. The decision of where to go is hers, however. It depends upon the congregation and on her husband's successor whether she can remain in the church community. I know of one congregation that has among its members the widows of three former pastors. This is surely a tribute to the wives or the congregation or the current pastor—or all three.

WHEN DEATH COMES

Gothic novels depend heavily upon the plight of orphaned and widowed clergy families for their plots. There is no doubt that economic factors have darkened the future for many clergy families in the past.

I have a dear friend whose clergyman father died in the mid-'40s when she was eighteen. It was before any pension plan and he left a mere $5,000 in life insurance—worth more then than today, but still not a large estate. She pays tribute to her mother, who with resourcefulness and business acumen, sold their possessions for top dollar. With the proceeds the mother was able to send my friend to a Philadelphia art school. With her daughter's schooling provided for, she began to think of herself. She wanted an education—denied her when she was younger. Through the advocacy of a church agency, she got a job as a housemother at a church-related college where she earned some academic credits. Transferring to a large university, and still working as a housemother, she received a dual degree in psychology and sociology when she was in her late fifties. She took a job with an urban welfare department and accrued social security benefits that made her somewhat independent until her death. It was a remarkable feat for a woman of her age, especially one with no societal economic support. She was well in advance of her time.

The clergy widow of today usually has better provisions made for her. (One large insurance company for religious professionals reports that the average amount of insurance that policyholders have with them has increased considerably over the past few years. The average-size policy the company writes is between $25,000 and $30,000. This does not indicate other insurance that may be carried.) The lesson to be learned from the story of the gallant woman told above is that life continues on. We have the chance to make it meaningful or to live in the past. To cherish and cling to our role as a clergy wife or to strike out in new and exciting directions.

Ours is a resurrection faith. Through Christ we are assured that in death there is life—in ending is beginning. This is a sustaining and hope-filled truth. It is a truth to cling to when we are faced with the death of a marriage.

Chapter VIII

The Search Goes On

There is an ancient truth that new occasions teach new duties. This is especially evident in the forms of ministry exercised by the church. These changed measurably from New Testament origins to the Reformation. So did the church's clergy. The monastic life gave way to the married pastoral minister. Alteration continued as doctrinal differences required varieties of gifts and roles in the pursuit of ministry. The ordination of women to the clergy gained momentum in the 1960's. It only seemed brand-new. Some major denominations had had clergywomen in 1940. Encouraged by the press for greater vocational choice and the amending of church polity, women sought ordination in increasing numbers.

Today there are many more women than ever before in seminaries and divinity schools. In recent years the percentage of women seminarians has risen from about 3 percent to 40 percent. These women, for the most part, plan to serve as full-time pastors of churches. Their reception into the ranks of the pastorate has been far from easy. Many women who seek ordination continue to find rejection because of their gender. It is interesting to note that one objection to the placement of clergywomen is that the traditional role of "minister's wife" is unfilled.

This is not wholly true, however, for many clergywomen are married. Their husbands are faced with a new and, in many ways, an undefined role. They are "clergy husbands" who may reject the traditional role because of its "super" female quality. No doubt they will face many of the dilemmas, concerns, and expectations of the clergy wife but from a different perspective. Writing in a magazine for ministers, one such spouse gives evidence of this likelihood. He notes his perception that the pastor's spouse is under a special type of self-discipline. What is said and done, even the manner of dress, must be in keeping with the pastor's vocation. Having heard this for years, he feels that in his role as a clergy husband, he now really understands. He even admits to a suspicion of being in competition with his wife's church. He closes by paying tribute to the tradition established by strong and wonderful clergy wives.

TEAM MINISTRIES

Another change occasioned by the entrance of women on the clergy "stage" is the increasing trend to husband-wife teams. "I'm the minister and the minister's wife too" is a description of the dual role some women are undertaking. A total of 750 clergy couple teams serve professionally in 13 Protestant denominations. It is realistic to expect that clergy teams will continue to rise with the increasing number of women seminarians.

There are several designs of employment for these couples. They may serve in one charge as co-pastors, in staff or agency positions, in separate churches or ministries with institutions, or only one partner may be employed. Within these arrangements there is diversity of time and salary distribution. Both may serve full time in salaried ministry, both part time, or with only one partner employed. Additionally, they must attempt to function equally in home maintenance. An increasing number are in a "shared ministry" with each spouse working part time. For example, one California couple has an interesting design. Each has two days off—one of them the same. They each receive three-quarters salary. Some observers feel that the great advantage of such pairings is that they represent a shared male/female model of ministry. On the other hand, it is pointed out that the clergy wife has previously provided the female aspect. The difference now is that the clergy wife as a clergywoman has training, status, and authority.

Finding employment is not an easy matter for clergy couple teams regardless of the pattern of ministry. Concerns on the part of the laity about family responsibilities is the major issue so far as the churches are concerned. For the clergy couple team, there is the problem of seeking the same type of job in a tight market or the need for geographically close positions. Often couples are forced by these realities to accept a position because they have no alternative. Clergywomen and couples who are both members of the clergy are nontraditional and face much pressure to conform to what is viewed as more acceptable forms. Undoubtedly, these new patterns represent valid ministries that will continue into the future.

There is in this trend, however, an observable danger. We can create "descending" classes of women who are related to the ministry. At the top would be the clergy husband/wife team with their unique, double relationship to the congregational and ecclesiastical systems. Next would be the clergywoman with her recognized status and pastoral role. At the very bottom would be the clergy wife. Some hint of this may be at the heart of current interest and concern.

The same occasions that have directed the assumption of new duties has affected the clergy wife. Three hundred and fifty years ago a book like this one would have depicted a segment of population that had no legal existence in England. It was not until 1604, under James I, that the marriage of clergy received state recognition. Mrs. Thomas Cranmer, wife of the first Archbishop of Canterbury, had to travel in a large box, carried on poles, the surface pierced with ventilating holes. The role definition for the clergy wife, through the generations since, has cramped the clergy wife like the traveling box of her predecessor. Consequently, clergy wives are seeking a new understanding of their singular variety of ministry.

CLARIFYING THE WIFE'S ROLE

Clergy wives must first honestly examine the methods of role definition. The women who marry ministers cannot alone determine the perimeters of their role. Many young women today say,

> "I have no role, I am not a minister's wife. I happen to be married to a man who is a minister."

This statement represents an exercise in semantics. It reflects an attempt to escape the realities of the situation. The man and the minister are one and the same. These realities are related to the nature of the ministry as a vocation. Ministry, for instance, can never be reduced to a forty-hour-a-week job. Certain personal sacrifices are required and the clergy wife must adjust to these.

The first and foremost factor in the development of the

wife's role is the husband. Again and again the clergy wives underscored their perception that they are first of all, wives —but the fact that their husbands are clergymen must be considered. The wife loves the man and she esteems the minister. Certainly, the fact that many marital problems and divorce are caused by "the wife's lack of support in his ministry" highlights his share in her role development. One young wife with eight and one half years in the parish says:

> "I am the wife of a man who chose to be a minister. I love him and he loves his job and is therefore very good at it. I could not ask him to give up that which he loves to do. We both love people, therefore I am interested in his vocation."

The second contributor to this role definition is the congregation. For the most part, their expectations are related to their perception of her share in the advancement of her husband's ministry. It is on this basis that the clergy wife enters into a relationship with the members of the congregation. When they share a common commitment to Christ and calling to mission, the relationship expresses a covenant. This is quite different from a congregation seeking to capitalize on her as a worker with little concern for her individuality. It is quite different, too, from a clergy wife who demands her rights for the best of opportunities, finances, and housing while minimizing her responsibilities for sharing and participation in ministry.

All of this underscores the need for open communication between the parties involved, particularly the minister and his wife. The clergy wife must be open to compromise and discussion in regard to her role and so must her spouse. Just as she cannot adopt a rigid definition that is unreal in its demands so she must guard against a rigid attitude of noninvolvement in terms of her own independence.

The commitment of the clergy wife entails, first of all, her devotion to Christ. It also includes loyalty to her husband and family, concern for others, particularly the congregation, and a sense of responsibility for her own development and self-expression. Her calling, like that of all Christians, places upon her the obligation to use and develop her talents in the service of God.

FACING UP TO ISSUES

The initial step in understanding the expectations in both her marriage and in the church life occurs during premarital counseling. It is easy for the pastor who marries a clergy couple to assume that they know the demands of marriage because of their acceptance of a vocational call to ministry. The opposite is true. They need specialized counseling that will aid them in exploring their assumptions and expectations about their ministry and their individual relationship to it and to each other. Since so many modern clergy couples are married when they enter seminary, it is the responsibility of the minister who officiates at their wedding to provide this distinctive pastoral guidance. It may even mean that the wedding will be canceled. A senior seminary student reported that his own engagement was broken when his fiancée was made aware of the realities of clergy marriage.

Most denominations have some administrative structure for the care and oversight of ministerial candidates. Sometimes this responsibility is assigned to a committee, sometimes to individuals, or it may be a combination of the two. Whatever the form of care, this is a very important time for the candidate and spouse in terms of change and growth.

Expectations on the part of both can be altered drastically by the educational and career influences which they experience. Close contact with the candidate is encouraged by ecclesiastical structures, but in most cases the spouse is not even known. It would be helpful if, during the seminary years, regular counseling dealing with communication between the husband and wife, priority and goal-setting, and reality confrontation be provided. Seminaries, with their resources of personnel and material, could incorporate such a program into the educational process or it could be under the aegis of judicatory representatives. At that level preventive therapy might help to reverse the growth of clergy marital unhappiness and divorce.

Congregations need to examine their attitudes and their part in the role development of the clergy wife. Repeatedly, the clergy wives requested some educational vehicle that would assist church members to view them as persons. In addition, there was a perceived need for the congregation to assess their legitimate and their unreal demands. Probably the best time for such examination occurs when a new pastor is called. Usually some type of self-study by the church is a part of the search for a new minister. Included in this exploration should be the congregational expectations of the clergy wife. Provided at this time should be an opportunity to better understand the needs of the clergy wife as a person and as a church member. This could be furnished through candid sharing by "third-party" minister's wives, personally or through tape or film.

During the years of ministry, many denominations are encouraging an annual review of pastoral needs and concerns, and of the job description and salary. The suggestion has been made by one wife that the congregation might also have such a review with the clergy wife, perhaps not yearly, but at regular intervals. If this is entered in the sense of mutual caring, it will provide valuable insight into the state of clergy-wife morale. Additionally, it would give evidence of any unfair congregational demands upon the spouse and the pastor. The provision of a "listening group" would be a valuable and caring ministry to the clergy wife.

As the clergy wife develops a new understanding of her role, she becomes aware of the need to enrich her contribution to it through training and education. Certainly the seminary years provide an unequaled opportunity to do so. With a growing consciousness of the effect of the clergy marriage upon ministry, it is not unrealistic for the seminaries and church-related colleges to be engaged in supplying some basic educational tools for the clergy wife. This could be done in the formal classroom at times when working wives are available, such as evenings or Saturdays or summer months. It could also be presented at seminars or informal programs during the year. It should be available not only to seminarian's wives but to those spouses who are already in the parish and feel the need for continuing education. However it is accomplished, it should include these emphases:

1. How to give support to the spouse and yet maintain personal identity;
2. The nature of ministry;
3. Basic theology;
4. Basic principles of Christian education and nurture;
5. Communication and conflict resolution.

The completion of such study should be recognized as an accredited level of education. This would implement the suggestion made by several wives that where the congregation expects the clergy wife to provide planning, leadership, and resource of church programs on a basis approaching a staff relationship, that she be paid for her time and ability as would any professional. There are many wives for whom this has no application, but there are many others who would find new dignity and fulfillment in such a relationship.

This emphasis upon enrichment and competence must encompass the spectrum of growth and development as a human being. There is strong evidence that the early years of ministry are the most difficult. Increasing maturity and the experience of coping with parish life solve many of these early problems for most women. Competence as a person involves not only one's abilities and training but their appropriate application to particular situations. Growth in that competence means knowing how to live and use one's life so that one does not burn oneself out in futile or undirected effort. It also means knowing how to renew and refresh oneself. Over and over the clergy wives expressed a desire for retreats, workshops, and informal opportunities to share this growth experience with one another and with their husbands. There is no question that specialized programs which recognize clergy-wife individuality will be of profit to the majority of clergy wives as they invest their time and themselves in ministry.

Some will receive great benefit from such meeting together. Others ask for a variety of helps to meet their personal needs. Some of these are in the form of written vehicles such as news letters, articles, and features for the clergy wife in church periodicals. These could be presented as "How I Coped" sharing and case studies that illustrate life-style or parenting solutions. The development of "self-help" literature is a possibility that would enable clergy wives to embark upon a course of study apart from a more formalized learning situation. This might include guidelines for clarifying the basis on which evaluation and decision are made. Instruction for financial planning is an often requested subject. Financing children's education and a knowledge of available scholarship help is important to parental concern. Clear understanding of pension and insurance benefits is vital for the retirement years as is comprehension of the widow's coverage in the event of the husband's death. Clergy wives need to be armed with information, skills, and investment guidance for coping with economic needs. Another suggested program element was an orientation to a new area of residence. It would outline the services and cultural and educational opportunities available.

HUMAN COUNSEL AND SUPPORT

Most support needs, however, must be supplied by human contact. The provision of social activities for clergy couples is a way to bridge the chasm of loneliness and isolation. These, in the past, have been both denominational and ecumenical in scope. Additionally, relationship with other clergy wives can fulfill some of the need for women friends. An assortment of pairings such as older couple to younger couple, older wife to younger wife—as a sort of "big sister" to her—can provide role models and solution-sharing. The provision by judicatories for a counseling service or persons to supply compassionate listening would be helpful.

The hiring of a clergy couple to serve the pastoral-care needs of ministers and families is more complicated. It certainly would be within the realm of possibility for a denomination, through an administrative unit, to do so. A local church council or association in larger communities could undertake such a ministry as an ecumenical venture. This position could be filled by a retired pastor. It also might be filled by a clergy couple team, thus meeting two needs—

pastoral care for minister's families and an additional opportunity for employment for a clergy couple team. The job description could assign responsibility for implementing the previously mentioned program elements as well as spiritual care and nurture.

As one looks at minister's wives, one is immediately aware of great diversity. What may be frustration for one is opportunity for another. What is a need for one is unnoticed or undesired by another. What is perceived as a part of her role by one is not even considered by another. What provides satisfaction and fulfillment for one proves a burden for another. The great common bond that unites them is their humanity and their engagement to be the Lord's. These they share with all of Christendom.

The clergy wife, if she is to find her true self, must not run away from life. She must live it as it actually is—in the church and in the world. If she is to grow, she must come to terms with imperfection both in herself and in those around her. Not that she becomes complacent, for she strives constantly for a more loving, more just order of things. In that struggle she loves—even those who disappoint or oppose. She expects frustration without losing heart. She learns to "run with patience," knowing that ultimate results rest with God.

In her sense of loneliness, she finds that within is the self which no other human can fully know or share. It is within her soul that she has fellowship with God. Strengthened by this sense of self and by the assurance of God's never-failing help, she does not despair in the face of human opinion or rejection.

The answer for the clergy wife, as for all others, is to be found in her relation to Jesus Christ and her commitment to him. The first response was made at the marriage altar. Here she bound her life to another in a covenant of love. Paul describes this covenant as a Christian unity marked by sacrifice, one for the other and for the family, as a parish where members find nurture and security, hope and love. In a further act of commitment, she may bind her life with her husband's in a call to ministry. For some this is found in a sense of partnership. As a seventy-three-year-old clergy wife said:

> "I wanted very much to contribute to the work of ministry and considered myself a teammate."

At the other end of life, a twenty-four-year-old clergy wife said:

> "Exciting, challenging, interesting, enlightening, demanding, full time and often overtime but never humdrum. I love my life and could use more hours a day to do for my Lord."

Though all may not feel such a clear sense of call, all would reject the demeaning view that they have been trapped by the circumstances of marriage in a life that is meaningless.

There is for all a sense of commitment to the Christ which is both "once and forever" and "day by day." The act of response is not defined by the fulfilling of a role. It is a Person-centered life that is a trusting dependence on the faithfulness of the Man—Jesus.

It was an act of love that called forth the giving of herself in marriage. It is an act of love that calls forth the giving of herself in ministry. The clergy wife is one who, for the love of a man—her husband—is a partner in love to THE Man —her Lord Jesus Christ. The giving of herself is a cherished gift to be held in honor and used by Him. So be it. Amen.

Selected Bibliography

Baldrige, Letitia. *Juggling: The Art of Balancing Marriage, Motherhood, and Career.* Viking Press, 1976.

Bjorn, Thyra Ferré. *Papa's Wife.* Rinehart & Co., 1955.

Bower, Robert K. *Solving Problems in Marriage: Guidelines for Christian Couples.* Wm. B. Eerdmans Publishing Co., 1972.

Davis, Jean Reynolds. *A Hat on the Hall Table.* Harper & Row, 1968.

De Beauvoir, Simone. *The Second Sex.* Trans. and ed. by H. M. Parshley. Alfred A. Knopf, 1971.

Dentler, Clara Louise. *Katherine Luther of the Wittenberg Parsonage.* United Lutheran Publishing House, 1924.

Denton, Wallace. *The Role of the Minister's Wife.* Westminster Press, 1962.

_____*The Minister's Wife as a Counselor.* Westminster Press, 1966.

Douglas, Ann. *The Feminization of American Culture.* Alfred A. Knopf, 1977.

Douglas, William Gray Thomson. *Ministers' Wives.* Harper & Row, 1965.

Hahn, Emily. *Once Upon a Pedestal.* Thomas Y. Crowell Co., 1974.

Harbeson, Gladys Evans. *Choice and Challenge for the American Woman.* Schenkman Publishing Co., 1967.

Howe, Reuel L. *Herein Is Love: A Study of the Biblical Doctrine of Love.* Judson Press, 1961.

Hudson, Robert Lofton. *'Til Divorce Do Us Part: A Christian Looks at Divorce.* Thomas Nelson, 1973.

Ibsen, Henrik. *A Doll's House.* Charles Scribner's Sons, 1906.

Jensen, Maxine Dowd. *The Warming of Winter.* Abingdon Press, 1977.

Lazareth, William H. *Luther on the Christian Home.* Muhlenberg Press, 1960.

Mace, David R. *Getting Ready for Marriage.* Abingdon Press, 1972.

Nye, Miriam Baker. *But I Never Thought He'd Die.* Westminster Press, 1978.

Oden, Marilyn Brown. *The Minister's Wife: Person or Position.* Abingdon Press, 1966.

Reeves, Nancy. *Womankind: Beyond the Stereotypes.* Aldine-Atherton, 1971.

Reische, Diana, ed. *Women and Society* (Vol. 43, No. 6, of *The Reference Shelf*). H. W. Wilson Co., 1972.

Sparks, James Allen. *Pot-shots at the Preacher.* Abingdon Press, 1977.

Street, James. *The High Calling.* Doubleday & Co., 1951.

Taves, Isabella. *Love Must Not Be Wasted: When Sorrow Comes.* Thomas Y. Crowell Co., 1974.

Truman, Ruth. *Underground Manual for Ministers' Wives.* Abingdon Press, 1974.

Winter, Gibson. *Love and Conflict: New Patterns in Family Life.* Doubleday & Co., 1958.

Wood, Miriam. *Two Hands, No Wings.* Review and Herald Publishing Association, 1968.